I0156991

# Practicing The Wisdom of Children
## Our Book Two

**For Sharing Unconditional Love & Nurturing True Friendship**

**By Understanding How My Mind Works**

By

William (Bill) Coulson

# Practicing The Wisdom of Children
## Our Book Two

**© 2019 by William Charles Coulson**

Library and Archives Canada Cataloguing
IBSN: 978-0-9813558-3-2

All rights reserved. No part of this book may be reproduced, stored in, or introduced into a retrieval system, or transmitted in any form, or by any means (electronic, mechanical, recording or otherwise), without the express written consent of the copyright owners, William Charles Coulson, a.k.a. Bill Coulson and Bill's son, Wil Coulson

Published by Coulson Press
Toronto Canada

Email: support@coulsonpress.com

Printing and Sales
by Amazon & Kindle

# Introduction to Our Book Two

## Understanding How My Mind Works

I have never been without a teacher. I study at the feet of our ancestors whose understanding of The Wisdom of Children fills my mind & body with the knowledge that I need to live my life with great passion, as our ancestors offer me the lessons that I need to learn to be worthy of living on Our Precious Earth, lessons that will increase the power of my unconditional love & forgiveness that I share with everyone in my life.

"The Wisdom of Children is the wisdom of using my childhood ability to share unconditional love & nurture true friendship. It is also the wisdom of accepting the love **from** all the life around me, especially the love from other human beings and the wisdom of embracing my love **for** all this life. This unconditional love of my childhood is a deep affection for the well-being of all the life on Our Precious Mother Earth. It is a love that lives continuously in my heart as it encourages me to take actions to help create, nurture, serve & protect the life that I observe & interact with each new day of my adult life, as I share this love with friends & family and they share their love with me. It is a powerful love that I was born possessing, a love that has been living inside me all my life, as it fuels my motivation to live my life with great passion."

(Quote from the Sharing Love & Adventures with Friends & Family section in Chapter 2 of Our Book One)

Why should I go outside myself in search of new wisdom to help me to live my life successfully, when I already have the empowering wisdom of our ancestors that I can study and begin to implement into my life, to achieve success in everything I do, with the help of other human beings who offer to share their love of new fun & adventures with me as we succeed together?

In this school of life that I am attending on our Precious Mother Earth, it is impossible to need a particular lesson for success without the lesson appearing. It is impossible for a lesson to appear without my needing it. The next lesson is ready and it is coming. The bucket containing the wisdom and a mop, for a new lesson, always appears on my pathway through life when I need it, to help me clean up any mess I make in my life or to help someone else clean up theirs.

God, My Creator, uses the wisdom of our ancestors to guide me and places a lesson of wisdom inside a bucket that sits on my pathway through life, so I will stumble over this bucket of wisdom, if necessary, when I do not seek new empowering wisdom to help me correct my faults & the mistakes I keep making in my adult life.

Each time I walk by without looking inside the bucket, my creator's purpose is to move the bucket a little closer to the middle of my path through life, so when I trip over the bucket and fall down, hopefully, this experience will jolt my mind into realizing that I should look inside the bucket at the wisdom that may help me to improve my life, provided that I practice this enhanced wisdom, enough, to validate that the wisdom will help me to stop making the same mistakes in my life, over & over again, in the future.

For each new challenge I face in life, I have two choices, the first choice is to pick up the mop from inside the bucket and start scrubbing to cleanse my mind of errors in my thinking as I start detaching from any life-diminishing feelings, thoughts & images that are trying to control me and the second choice is to push the bucket of helpful wisdom out of my pathway and say I don't need to understand this.

When I am ready for the wisdom of our ancestors to benefit my future life, this wisdom will come to me automatically, even if I do not seek it.

However, when I am not ready for the wisdom of our ancestors, I will not be able to understand it, even if it is sitting inside a book that lies open to the page of wisdom that I want to learn, as I try to understand the wisdom that lies in front of me.

To become ready for the wisdom of our ancestors to grace my future life, I must first become able to understand how my mind works, so I can ask my mind to help me understand this wisdom before I can apply this wisdom to my future life.

Understanding how my mind works helps me to connect with the Internal Source of Unconditional Love that lives inside me, a love that I was born possessing that enables me to live my life with great passion.

Understanding how my mind works increases my ability to share unconditional love & nurture true friendship with everyone in my life.

Understanding how my mind works increases my pure personal power to take self-disciplined action to complete all the goals for my life.

And understanding how my mind works enables me to practice The Nine Steps to Emotional Freedom from unresolved pain & suffering that my unfair memories, my ego or the new events in my life may create inside my conscious mind during the day, to enable me to replace this pain & suffering with increasing love & joy.

Please read My Son's summary of The Nine Steps to Emotional Freedom from unresolved pain & suffering, as he offers you the wisdom of our ancestors in his own words, as he describes how his mind works to enable him to share love & joy with his friends & family.

## My Son Wil's Wisdom for Practicing The Nine Steps to Emotional Freedom

"I'm a sailor in a boat of my own construction, riding on a sea of uncontrolled feelings. I can continue to drift aimlessly with the current from wave to wave of changing feelings, hopefully enjoying my feelings or just surviving the pain of whatever negative feeling comes my way. Or I can upgrade my boat, install a motor, pull out a map, and navigate through the waves of feeling until I reach a new destination where the sea gently rocks my boat with continuous undulating waves of love and joy.

What defines my life in this sea of feelings? What sets my direction? What controls the nature, speed and direction of the waves of feeling?

To a great extent my life on this sea of feelings is defined by my fears that are given strength by the pain I've accumulated in my memories. What would it be like to be fearless? To set my direction without worrying about what might happen? Truly unlocking my potential for increasing the love and joy in my life requires me to kill the pain in my memories. I can kill the pain carried by the waves of feeling that are created inside my memories by following nine steps:

**Step 1 - Practicing Detachment**

Everything I've ever not wanted to do, I've not wanted to do because of the pain present in my memories related to that thing I've not wanted to do. They say there's a reason that work is called work and play is called play. Work isn't supposed to be fun. It's just something that I don't want to do but do anyway because it's necessary for me to do so. But what if that wasn't the case? What if I at least was indifferent about what work was and at most was allowed to become excited about it by learning to kill any pain associated with doing it.

Thus, it's evident that everything material in my life forms a blank slate onto which I project my feelings. My bias towards things, the way I feel about them, is dictated by my past experiences with them. My preconceptions and misconceptions are made by assuming that future experiences will be exactly like past experiences, and that furthermore, my past experiences, and the ways I felt about them, were completely valid and true. Believing, in this way, that the future will be just like the past, and that my memories of the past are completely accurate, means that I'm doomed to take life like I always have, repeating the same mistakes, and accepting positive change very slowly, if at all.

Freeing me from the rigidity caused by my fear of the waves of pain that I may encounter on the sea of my feelings requires that I practice detachment. Detachment is the process through which I separate me from my feelings. Doing so allows me to realize that the way I feel about a situation has little to do with my present reality and more to do with the pain present within my memories. When my present situation reminds me of painful memories of similar situations in my past, I make the emotional connection and thus magnify and intensify my negative thoughts and feelings. To remove this mechanism's power over me I must detach from my feelings and realize that I can control how I feel.

## Step 2 - Practicing Friendship

After practicing detachment, my next step to emotional freedom is practicing friendship. Making friends with the pain in my memories allows me the opportunity to gain the knowledge to improve my ability to practice detachment. When I find myself in a situation in which my memories are causing me excessive pain, rather than allow the pain from those memories to overwhelm me, I take the opportunity to understand where the pain is coming from and why my memories are causing me pain. Detaching and understanding my pain from an emotional distance allows me to further realize and reinforce that the pain from my memories needn't control me. I can control the way I feel about any situation by making my feelings my friends because how I feel about a situation is up to me.

## Step 3 - Practicing Control of My Mind

The easiest way to detach from distractions that may try to take control of my mind is to practice meditation when I work on my goals for today. Meditation is practicing detachment from all the distractions in my mind that are preventing me from achieving mindfulness. Mindfulness is a state of awareness in which I'm aware of everything that's happening around me. I spend most of my life daydreaming, wrapped up in my feelings, constantly thinking, and unaware of the present moment. My feelings control me the most when I'm daydreaming.

When I meditate and achieve a state of mindfulness I detach from my thoughts and feelings. This creates mental space in which I can start practicing control of my mind by using my reasoning ability to control how I feel and act towards my present situation. Thus, when presented with a difficult situation, I withdraw from it by hitting my meditative trigger. For me it's taking notice of the objects around me that I had been previously ignoring. A meditative trigger can be anything that allows me to achieve a state of mindfulness. Hitting my meditative trigger and meditating for a moment allows me to detach from any distractions that may enter my mind and try to stop me working on my goals for today.

## Step 4 - Practicing Fairness

By practicing control of my mind I am able to treat all human beings equally with the same love and forgiveness that I am offering my friends & family. As I think about the situations I face in life, I can build a positive habit of facing pain with detachment by believing that my future life will become fair to me. Thus, I become better and better at practicing fairness and friendship as I gain emotional knowledge and meditative experience. My memories cause me less pain and my feelings control me less.

## Step 5 - Practicing Forgiveness

Unfairness is the most powerful negative feeling that stems from my memories. Thus, practicing forgiveness is very important when assessing the situations I find myself in, in life and when evaluating the validity of the feelings I feel when reliving my memories. When I experience unfairness in a present situation, I detach from my feelings of fear or anger. When a present situation reminds me of a past situation where I was treated unfairly, I detach from the feelings of fear or anger that I feel as a result of my memory. Detaching in this way requires me to forgive those people who have treated me unfairly in the past and to forgive the forces of nature that may be treating me unfairly in the present. I realize that my emotional reaction has little relevance to reality and little impact on outcomes. Detaching from my emotional response to unfairness by forgiving the cause of that unfairness allows me to diminish my pain both now and in the future.

## Step 6 - Choosing My Feelings

The key benefit of detachment is realizing that I am not my feelings. Going through life, it is very easy for my feelings to dictate my every action. Emotionally, I will strive with all my actions to pursue pleasure and to avoid pain. Living emotionally in this way causes me to settle in a physical state that resonates with my emotional state. Thus, I can find myself statically indulging my pleasures while avoiding work that may be painful that would lead to improvement.

Long term improvement in my life comes from achieving my goals. This is because achievement allows me to move to a higher level of physical and emotional resonance as I learn to choose the feelings that I want to experience.

## Step 7 - Practicing Self-Discipline

Enduring the pain of physical exercise improves my body and allows for me to experience higher levels of physical achievement and greater levels of physical pleasure in the future. While detaching from pleasure is important in order to maintain emotional control, it is possible to enjoy pleasure while detaching. This is because detaching while experiencing pleasure allows me to control, yet still experience, positive feeling.

After exercising, my entire being is enhanced. The benefits far exceed the costs of the work I put in. However, I often don't exercise because I have negative feelings towards work. By detaching through meditation and mindfulness when my negative feelings are preventing me from exercising, I realize that the work I put in is minimal and the benefits I receive in return are great in the long term. I accomplish my goals by making my negative feelings my friend and by allowing them to teach me about my emotional mechanism. I forgive myself for having negative feelings and treating me unfairly in the past when I allowed my negative feelings to prevent me from exercising.

By taking these steps I choose my feelings and allow myself to achieve my goals, such as exercising. Practicing Self-Discipline to achieve my goals pushes me to higher and higher levels of physical and emotional resonance. In this way I can improve my existence, minimize my emotional costs, and maximize my emotional benefits.

## Step 8 - Practicing Thankfulness

Practicing thankfulness helps me to become inherently joyous and loving. Once I've detached, befriended, forgiven, and managed the negative feelings in my memories that were preventing me from accomplishing my goals, I'm ready to thank. Being thankful is the exercise through which I strengthen my connection to the universal source of love and joy. Similar to how exercising by doing squats helps me to run faster; being thankful helps me to be more loving and joyous.

There are many things to be thankful for and they are easy to recognize once my mind is free of negativity. Being alive is wondrous and on top of that is celebrating my love for living in a world filled with unconditionally loving people.

## Step 9 - Sharing All The Love in The Universe

I possess within me a permanent connection to the universal source of love and joy. I was born with an uninterrupted connection to this source. However, over the years I've been increasingly cut off from it by the accumulation of pain in my memories through negative experiences.

The ultimate goal of gaining freedom from my painful feelings is to allow me to reignite my permanent connection to the universal source of love and joy.

Taking The Nine Steps to Emotional Freedom allows me to free myself from my emotional prison of negativity. Like a prisoner behind bars, I can't realize what I'm missing in the world outside until I take steps in the right direction towards increasing the love, peace and joy in my life, as I walk outside of my self-imposed prison of negative painful memories that I have been allowing to control my life and keep me in prison, afraid to work on new challenges and afraid to make changes in my life because I may fail. Now I am becoming fearless, as I practice Choosing My Feelings, as I bring continuous love, peace and joy into my life from all the life in the universe that I share with my friends and family, by taking control of my feelings to enable me to choose my future life and my future destiny."

(Quote from My Son Wil's Wisdom for Practicing The Nine Steps section in Chapter 15 of Our Book One)

**What Am I Asking My Mind to Do, When I Practice The Nine Steps?**

"The answer to this question empowers my mind with the mental tools that I need to practice The Nine Steps to Emotional Freedom from unresolved pain & suffering, which enable me to experience continuous love, peace, joy & compassion during every moment of every day of my adult life. (Please refer to Question 58 in the Questions to Answer in My Own Words section in Chapter 31 of Our Book One)

Today, my first challenge to achieve emotional freedom started this morning when I decided to detach from my dreams, so I could wake up and use the understanding of how my mind works to choose to fully reconnect with the continuous love, peace joy & compassion flowing through me from all the life in the universe, and then use these life enhancing feelings to help motivate me to share new fun & adventures with those I love, today.

My second challenge was to get out of bed and start my Aerobics, Yoga & Strength Training Exercises to help my mind & body function at their full potential.

After exercising, I observed how my mind & body were feeling by measuring the level of my mental & physical energy that is available to me today, as I began enjoying my feelings of well-being that my morning exercises have helped bring into my life.

Then, I started thinking about the goals for my life as I reviewed my mental list of potential goals for today before showering, as I gauged how many of the goals I could accomplish today.

After breakfast, I started working on my first new goal and I started adding thinking power to my desire to accomplish all my goals for today, as I began to look forward to increasing my feelings of being worthy of living as I accomplish each goal during the day.

Now, I am spending the rest of today working on my goals and continuously loving my friends, family & all the life on Our Precious Mother Earth, which is made possible by the enhanced wisdom of our ancestors, as I continue to practice The Nine Steps to Emotional Freedom to enable me to choose the feelings of love & inspiration that I want to experience today.

To continue my challenge of achieving emotional freedom today, I am asking my mind to help me to choose the feelings that I want to experience instead of allowing unfair painful feelings or other distractions to gain control of my mind, as I continue practicing The Nine Steps to Emotional Freedom, as my understanding of how my mind works helps me to fully reconnect to my internal source of continuous love, peace, joy & compassion that is living inside me.

**When I Ask My Mind to help me practice The Nine Steps to Emotional Freedom during each moment of every new day of my life:**

**1) I am Practicing Detachment** to stop my distractions from trying to control me.

I am asking my mind to help me practice meditation & mindfulness, so I can calm my mind enough to become able to **spot** any new distractions that may enter my mind, as these new feelings, thoughts & images try to distract me from working on my goals.

And then, I am asking my mind to use my reasoning & decision making abilities to find a way to **detach** from these new distractions, as quickly as possible, so I can stop them from trying to control me, to enable me to return to using the full power of my mental creativity to accomplish my goals.

Even though Buddhists call a fully detached mind, as achieving the mental state of An Eternal Mind, I prefer to call a fully detached mind as achieving the mental state of Becoming A Compassionate Watcher who has the ability to detach from & then control all the feelings, thoughts & images in my conscious mind, to enable me to choose the life enhancing feelings thoughts & images that I want to experience in my life and to enable me to kill the life diminishing feelings, thoughts & images in my conscious mind that I do not want to continue experiencing. (Please refer to a Buddhist text, such as Complete Enlightenment by Ch'an Master Sheng-yen, for a more detailed understanding of the concept of An Eternal Mind)

**2) I am Practicing Friendship** with my feelings, thoughts & images to understand why they are living inside my mind.

I am asking my mind to help me make friends with the powerful feelings, thoughts & images that I will experience today, so each feeling, thought or image will be encouraged by this new friendship to tell me why a memory, my ego, or an event in my life created this powerful feeling, thought or image to live inside my conscious mind.

Then, I am using the understanding of why these powerful feelings, thoughts & images are being created and why they are living inside my conscious mind, so I can empower the life enhancing feelings that are motivating me to work on my goals and so I can kill the life diminishing feelings that are beginning to hurt me.

**3) I am Controlling My Mind** to accomplish my goals for today.

I am asking my mind to help me achieve the mental state of a fully detached mind as I become A Compassionate Watcher who controls all my feelings, thoughts & images, as I choose the actions that I will take today, as my memories, my ego & the external events in my life create the ever changing feelings, thoughts & images that will enter my conscious mind today, as they live with me for a while, and then as they disappear from my conscious mind & body, later today.

As these feelings, thoughts & images try to influence the choices that I am making during the day, I begin to detach from all of them unless one of them offers to help me to work on the goals that I am trying to accomplish today, as I maintain Control of My Mind to work on my goals, as my motivation flows from my internal source of unconditional love that is living inside me.

**4) I am Practicing Fairness** to enable my future life to be fair to me.

The Power of Fairness is the ability that I was born possessing which enables my adult life to be fair to me in the future, as long as I practice The Nine Steps to Emotional Freedom.

I am asking my mind to help me practice fairness by treating all human beings equally with the same love & forgiveness that I offer my friends & family.

And I am asking My Mind to help me kill any unfairness that is living inside me to restore the long term fairness in my life.[14]

So, when my memories, My Ego or new external events in my life generate new unfair anger, fear, worry & stress inside my conscious mind because they believe that life may be unfair to me in the future, I tell them that they are wrong and I tell them that my future life will be filled with fairness, because I believe that fairness is only way that human beings can work together successfully, so that all human beings can benefit from our accomplishments, as this desire for increased fairness in our lives motivates us to stop any neurotic unfair human beings who may try to prevent us from working together as their neurosis begins to create pain & suffering in our lives.

All human beings are born with the desire to create fairness as shown by our collective desire to elect politicians, who we give our trust, to help pass new laws that will bring increased justice & fairness into our lives.

Even though there is a lot of unfairness in the world, my mind has the ability to convince my memories, My Ego or new external events in my life that my future life will be fair to me and to my friends & family.

So, when I am able to convince a memory, My Ego or a new external event in my life that my future life will be fair to me, it will stop generating new feelings of unfairness inside my conscious mind, such as anger, fear, worry or stress and my mind will start to become peaceful, once again.

In other words, a memory, My Ego or a new external event in my life will believe that life will be fair to me in the future, as long as I can convince it that the unfair experience that was created in my life, will not occur again in the future.

Though new unfair events may still create pain in my future life, I am learning what is creating this new unfairness when it enters my life, so I can kill this unfairness quickly to help restore the long term fairness in my life that will bring feelings of increasing love, peace, joy & compassion back into my life.

**5) I am Practicing Forgiveness** to unblock the pathway to my internal source of love, peace, joy & compassion.

I am fully re-connecting to my internal source of unconditional love by asking my mind to help me forgive those who created painful experiences in my past life.

Forgiveness takes away my mind's need to generate new pain into my future life because it no longer needs to use pain to get my attention so it can tell me that my future life may be unfair to me, as it has been in the past, because it now accepts that my future life will be fair to me for long periods of time in the future because I have forgiven those who created this pain in my past life and because my mind now believes that these previously unfair human beings will not hurt me again in the future.

So now that I have used forgiveness to convince my mind that my life will be fair in the future, my mind will no longer be motivated to generate new pain into my life that will block the pathway to my internal source of unconditional love.

Then, as this pathway becomes clear of the unresolved pain & suffering that was living inside my conscious mind, I begin to feel continuous love, peace, joy and compassion which is being generated inside my subconscious mind, a powerful unconditional love from my childhood that I was born possessing and that has been flowing inside me during every moment of every day of my life, from childhood until now.

**6) I am Choosing My Feelings** that I want to experience & I am killing my feelings that try to hurt me.

As I fully reconnect with My Internal Source of Unconditional love that lives inside me, I become able to ask my mind to help me choose my feelings that I want to experience in my life, as I observe all my feelings that live inside me, as I choose to feel the childhood love, peace, joy and compassion which is being generated by my internal source of powerful unconditional love, feelings that I can use to increase the power of the living thinking energy in my conscious mind to help me kill any negative feelings, thoughts or images that may try to hurt me or block the pathway to the source of my life-enhancing feelings of unconditional love, friendship & forgiveness.

**7) I am Practicing Self-Discipline** to share unconditional love & forgiveness with everyone in my life.

Self-discipline is the ability to make myself do things that I know I should do even when I do **not** want to do them. (Cambridge English Dictionary)

I am practicing Self-Discipline to enable me to continuously think that my life will be fair to me in the future, to enable My Internal Source of Unconditional Love to motivate me to continuously share unconditional love & forgiveness with everyone in my life.

And practicing Self-Discipline enables me to detach from all the feelings, thoughts & images that are trying to control my mind, so I can use My Free Will to choose my feelings that I want to experience.[17]

**8) I am Practicing Thankfulness** to nurture true friendship with everyone in my life.

I am asking my mind to help me thank the members of my friends & family who have been supporting me with encouragement, hope, sympathy, forgiveness & unconditional love, as I start to fully appreciate how much I love them and how much I owe them for their support, as I use my re-acquired childhood ability to share increasing love, peace, joy & compassion with them, feelings that are being continuously generated by the internal source of unconditional love that is living inside me.

**9) I am Sharing All the Love in the Universe** to recharge my internal source of unconditional love.

I am asking my mind to help me to use meditation & mindfulness to maintain a **continuous** connection to all the love in the universe that is flowing through me during every moment of every day of my adult life to enable this powerful love to continually recharge My Internal Source of Unconditional Love that lives inside me.

As I continue to practice the nine steps, I see nothing in my friends & family but their childhood ability to love everyone in their lives with great passion, no matter how diminished their ability may be at the present time, as I prepare to embrace their love today, as I continue to love them, and as I prepare to forgive them for any unfair pain & suffering they may create in my life.

Then each morning, after I mentally review the Nine Steps, I ask myself three additional questions:

**1) Can I remember when I felt immense love for all the life around me, when I was a young child, as I shared new fun & adventures with my family & friends? Q-1**

The answer to this question helps me to realize that I was born to live my life with great passion, which increases my motivation to fully reconnect with this childhood ability to feel immense love during each moment of every new day of my adult life.

**2) Will I pay any price that is required to fully reconnect to the passion of my childhood, to enable me to feel continuous love, peace, joy & compassion in my adult life? Why? Q-5**

The answer to this question helps me to realize that there may be temporary adversity & pain in my life as I accomplish My Goals for Today, as I begin to realize that the price of this suffering is worth paying, to be able to continue loving everyone in my life with great passion, as I accomplish my goals which will help me to serve & protect those I love.

Practicing the wisdom of The Nine Steps to Emotional Freedom "helps us to learn meditation & mindfulness techniques to enable us to understand how our minds **actually** work and then enables us to understand how our minds **should** work, to help us correct the errors in our thinking, as we use our reasoning ability to control the thinking energy that we use to power our joyful life enhancing feelings, especially to empower the motivation to accomplish the goals for our lives."

And I believe that the Primary Goal for our lives as human beings living on Our Precious Mother Earth is "to increase the love, peace, joy & compassion in our daily lives by learning how to kill the unresolved pain & suffering that is buried in our old unfair memories that many of us keep reliving each day of our adult lives, as we try to fully reconnect to the Internal Source of Unconditional Love of our childhood, a connection that we were born possessing and that many of us have diminished or lost.

When we fully reconnect to our childhood ability to live our lives with great passion, we start to experience the **continuous** love, peace, joy & compassion that we remember experiencing when we were children." (Modified quotes from the Overview of the Wisdom in Our Book Series section in Chapter 5 of Our Book One)

### 3) What have I learned from practicing The Nine Steps to Emotional Freedom?

The answer to this question helps me realize that I have practiced the wisdom in Our Book One, well enough, to learn how to detach from all the feelings, thoughts & images that will go through my mind during each new moment of today, as I observe all the events that are happening in my life, such as the activities of my friends, family, co-workers, and other human beings, who I will share love & friendship with today.

As I detach, I am looking at the new feelings, thoughts & images that are being created by the new events in my life today, as these feelings, thoughts & images enter my conscious mind, stay with me for a while, and then eventually disappear from my mind, later today.

I do **not** try to change them or control them as they pass through my mind.

However, I do decide which ones will help motivate me to work on My Goals for Today and I am adding my living thinking energy to the life promoting feelings to prolong their lives as they sojourn inside my mind, by telling myself that life is being fair to me, as I try to fully understand how they will benefit me before they leave my mind.

The unwanted feelings, thoughts & images, whose nature & purpose I can identify, I leave alone without trying to change them or control them, until they run out of the living energy they brought with them when they entered my mind.

And I do **not** give them any new thinking energy that will keep them alive inside my mind, by **not** telling myself that life is being unfair to me, whenever one of these unwanted feelings, thoughts or images generates new worry, stress, pain, suffering, fear or angry inside my mind, whenever someone treats me unfairly or when I start to relive a painful unfair memory.

I am refusing to indulge in feeling the unfairness or the pain by mentally detaching from these unwanted mental distractions, as they try to control me, until they run out of the energy they are using to stay alive inside my mind.

Then, I begin to feel increasing **peace**, as these unwanted, distracting and sometimes hurtful feelings, thoughts & images stop diminishing my motivation to work on my goals today, as they start to die from lack of energy and begin to disappear from my conscious mind.

As these unwanted distractions disappear from my mind, empty space is created inside my conscious mind, which starts to fill up with the unconditional love that lives in my subconscious mind because the pathway to this love is no longer being blocked by the unresolved pain & suffering that these unwanted feelings, thoughts & images brought into my conscious mind, unwanted distractions that are no longer living inside me.

In summary, asking my mind for help is a continuous ongoing mental process that starts each morning, when I wake up, as I start to receive the 60.000 + feelings, thoughts & images that will go through my mind each day and as I start practicing Step One of The Nine Steps to Emotional Freedom by using my living thinking energy to detach from all my feelings, thoughts & images that are living inside my conscious mind, so I can begin to understand each new life enhancing feeling, thought & image and I can begin to understand each new life diminishing mental distraction, as each one of them enters my mind and then tries to get my mental attention; so it can convince me to do something, to observe something, to feel something, or to help me understand the message which it brought with it, when it entered my conscious mind.

And when I make mistakes during the day, as I try to implement the nine steps into my life, I do **not** tell myself that I am unworthy of living. Instead, I tell myself that I am worthy of living because I was born with the ability to correct my mistakes, to learn from my mistakes, and then choose to use this new learning to **not** make the same mistakes again in the future.

In this way, The Nine Steps to Emotional Freedom from Our Book One enable me to choose the feelings, thoughts & images that I want to experience each day and enable me to Kill those that are of no help to me, especially the ones that try to hurt me, de-motivate me, or distract me from working on my goals during each new day of my life, goals which are important to me, such as working of projects that help me earn a living, or help me to love friends & family more, or help me to share new fun & adventures with those I love."

(Quote from the What Am I Asking My Mind to Do, when I Practice The Nine Steps section in Chapter 14 of Our Book One)

Only by practicing the wisdom in Our Book One am I becoming able to fully benefit from the enhanced wisdom in Our Book Two that My Creator puts inside the bucket of wisdom that is sitting on my pathway through life, as I take the mop from the bucket of wisdom to cleanse my mind of errors in my thinking and to cleanse my mind of any new life-diminishing feelings, thoughts or images, to enable me to feel increased love, peace, joy and compassion in my life each day, life-enhancing feelings that are becoming a **continuous** stream of unconditional love that I am sharing with all the life that surrounds me, as I look out into the world and as I choose the fun & adventures that I want to experience today.

(Please refer to The Nine Steps to Emotional Freedom section in Chapter 13 of Our Book One)

**Forgiving Others Who Do Not Deserve Forgiveness**

"In addition to the wisdom of sharing unconditional love, Our Book One contains the wisdom of forgiving others who do not deserve forgiveness.

Forgiveness enables me to kill the unresolved pain & suffering that is living inside my unfair memories.

Unfortunately, my old friends & family members created many of these painful memories when they treated me unfairly, as I grew from childhood into adulthood.

This old pain & suffering automatically starts to come out of hiding from inside my unfair memories when it re-enters my daily adult life, as new pain & suffering, whenever someone treats me unfairly again in the future. The power & intensity of this new pain & suffering is determined by the number of unfair memories that are awakened inside me when I experience a new unfairness in my future life that is similar to the experiences contained in some of my old unfair memories.

Then, when the new pain & suffering, that is generated by my old memories, builds inside my conscious mind until it becomes intense, I may lash out with new angry words or deeds that hurt the loved ones in my life, when I start looking for an excuse to release the new pain & suffering from inside me, to allow it to escape from me into the external world of people & events that surround me. This lashing out at another person, as I become abusive, allows me to reduce the stress of living with the new pain & suffering from my old memories.

Unfortunately, after this pain & suffering of the moment leaves my mind & body to go live inside the new memories that I have just created inside a friend or family member who I have hurt with my angry words or deeds, I may utter an excuse for hurting this person by saying "My pain & suffering is justified because you have treated me unfairly", without realizing that I have also treated this person unfairly by adding extra pain & suffering from my old memories to the amount of hurt that I poured upon the person who I blamed for creating the new unfairness in my life.

At this time, I may not realize that the intensity of my new pain & suffering has been increased unfairly by the power of my old unfair memories when they generated extra pain & suffering into my conscious mind, when they were awakened from sleep inside my subconscious mind because these memories contain experiences similar to the experience of the new unfair event that just occurred. It may be later when I use meditation to understand this new unfair experience that I realize I treated another person unfairly.

Relieving our daily stress by abusing friends & family members, in this way, can become an addictive bad habit in our adult lives, which we discuss in more detail in the Abusing Friends & Family section in Chapter 13 of Our Book One.

All of us endure stress in our daily lives when we work at our jobs, take care of our children, or help loved ones who need us.

Unfortunately, many of us carry around a bag of unresolved pain & suffering in our lives that adds to the amount of stress that we feel during the day.

To help you to understand this, please imagine a couple who have been living together for ten years, when one partner asks the other, "Why do I **not** feel the same intensity of love & excitement in our relationship today that I felt 10 years ago?"

In reply, the other partner says, "It is partially my fault because I have disappointed you so many times over the last 10 years that these unfair experiences have built up unresolved pain & suffering inside your memories, which diminish the love that you feel for me, whenever you relive one or more of these unfair memories of the many times that I have disappointed you.

So now, when I come home from work and you look at me as I enter the front door, some of this unresolved pain & suffering may enter your conscious mind and reduce the power of your feelings of love for me.

Unfortunately, I do not know how to help you kill this unresolved pain & suffering that is living inside your memories, so it can no longer diminish the power of your love.

I have asked you to forgive me many times in our relationship, but I do not know how our minds create forgiveness and I do not know how our minds can help us to kill the unresolved pain & suffering in our memories that we carry around with us each day.

So, please try to forgive me once again and add this new failure of my not knowing how to help, to the bottom of the long list of disappointments that I have created in your life.

During each new day of sharing my life with you, I am blessed by your continuous love and I treasure your ongoing ability to live with my many imperfections. You are the love of my life who I do not want to disappoint, so I will keep trying to be more caring, more understanding and more attentive to your needs."

This imaginary relationship illustrates why I need to learn how to forgive my friends & family members whenever they do not deserve my forgiveness, so I can kill the old pain & suffering that still lives inside me, so I do not allow this old pain & suffering to reduce the power of the love that I feel for my friends & family.

When I try to kill this unresolved pain & suffering, I do not need to use forgiveness to benefit the friends & family members who created the painful unfair events of my childhood and who may be creating more unfairness in my adult life. And I do not have to tell them that I have forgiven them, though that would help me to forgive. What I need to do is forgive them whenever I think of them, which will prevent the old pain & suffering from awakening inside my old painful memories of unfairness that is still living inside my subconscious mind and which will prevent my old memories from generating new pain & suffering inside my conscious mind, whenever I am treated unfairly again in the future.

Unfortunately, as I grew up, my memories of unfair pain & suffering began to grow in number & intensity as they started to live together inside my subconscious mind to become the thousands of memories of unfairness that are still living inside me today. Memories that will still hurt me and hurt my friends & family today, when they contain remnants of the old unresolved pain & suffering from the unfair painful experiences that I endured during my lifetime, whenever a new unfair event in my future life opens the door to My Room of Memories in my subconscious mind, when I give my old memories an excuse to enter my adult life, as I start to blame my friends & family for this old unresolved pain & suffering whenever one of my friends or a family member starts to treat me unfairly again in my future life.

To help me to visualize the amount of new unresolved pain & suffering that is being generated into my life each day by these old unfair memories, I use my mind to imagine me carrying around A Bag of Unresolved Pain & Suffering that is being refilled each day of adult life, whenever I start to relive one of these old unfair painful memories.

For many years I carried around this bag of unresolved pain & suffering, which contained feelings of resentment, feelings of unfairness, and unresolved fear, anger, worry & stress, as it diminished my ability to feel the full power of the unconditional love that has been living inside me since I was born.

As a child, I continually looked inside my mind as I tried to understand how it worked, so I could use this understanding to find answers to my questions about the behavior of friends & family that puzzled me, when I could not understand why they were acting this way.

I was also puzzled as a child when I did not understand why every human being that I knew was carrying around A Bag of Unresolved Pain & Suffering that they did not know how to empty, which if emptied, would allow them to bring more joy into their lives.

Unfortunately, some of them carried around large bags of unresolved pain & suffering that prevented them from loving anyone because they were in continuous pain & suffering which they tried to hide from their friends & family, as they sought to relieve their pain & suffering for short periods of time through excessive use of alcohol, drugs, or promiscuous sexual encounters, etc. or by being abusive to a friend or family member to help relieve the stress of this unresolved pain & suffering whenever it was generated inside their conscious mind by an old unfair painful memory that they started reliving.

Fortunately, others carried around small bags of unresolved pain & suffering that barely diminished their ability to love everyone in their life.

Unfortunately, I could not help my friends & family because I did not know how to kill the pain & suffering that I was carrying around with me, until I studied the wisdom of our ancestors who provided me with answers that I could use to kill my unresolved pain & suffering. This wisdom taught me how to use forgiveness to kill the pain & suffering that was being generated by the old unfair memories that I was reliving each day of my life. I wanted to kill the ability of these old memories to generate new pain & suffering into my daily life, so they could not hurt me again in the future and so they could not hurt those I love.

Then, after I practiced this wisdom and the killing was done, my bag of unresolved pain & suffering became empty and it remained empty, until someone hurt me unfairly again in the future. Then, I used forgiveness to kill this new pain & suffering that had just entered my life.

And I killed my new desire for justice & revenge that encouraged me to force the person who had just hurt me to pay me compensation in remorseful words, deeds or money for this new unfairness. This killing process, which included knowing how to use my mind to forgive, enabled me to empty my bag of unresolved pain & suffering, once again

When I was a young child, I was taught to use forgiveness when I attended a Christian Sunday School, however this Christian teaching did not enable me to understand how my mind worked, so I was not able to implement The How to Forgive Process into my mind so I could become able to use forgiveness as often as I wanted to, during my childhood.

It was not until I studied Buddha's wisdom, many years later, that I learned how my mind worked, which enabled me to use forgiveness to kill all the unresolved pain & suffering that was living inside my mind in my bag of unresolved pain & suffering.

And Buddha taught me to replace this unresolved pain & suffering with unconditional love that automatically entered into my conscious mind, when I used Buddhist wisdom to choose the feelings that I wanted to experience, after I had cleansed my mind of my old unresolved pain & suffering by tapping into the full power of my Internal Source of Unconditional Love, a continuous love that allows me to forgive others who have treated me unfairly in the past, a continuous love that automatically kills the unresolved pain & suffering in my memories when I forgive others, and a continuous love that has been living inside me since I was born, but which unfortunately, may be partially hidden from me or blocked by new pain & suffering when it enters my conscious mind, whenever I relive an old unfair memory that I have not cleansed with my forgiveness.

Buddha's wisdom is also helping me to become A Compassionate Watcher each morning, as I use Buddhist meditation techniques to observe all the feelings, thoughts & images that live in my conscious mind, as they continuously compete for control of my mind & actions during the day, as My Compassionate Watcher enables me to mentally detach from all my feelings, until I decide to choose the feelings that I want to experience and until I decide to kill the feelings that I no longer want to experience, by maintaining control of my mind with my reasoning ability, which allows My Compassionate Watcher to use forgiveness to stop an old memory from generating new pain & suffering into my future life and which allows My Compassionate Watcher to extend the life expectancy of the feelings that I want to experience.

Unfortunately, you may have to reread this section of our book several times, to completely understand this wisdom, to enable you to bring increasing love & joy into your life.

To help you understand the wisdom for forgiving the unresolved pain & suffering in our lives, I asked My Son Wil to explain his understanding of this wisdom to help you to rewrite this wisdom in your own words, to make it easier for you to explain this wisdom to your friends & family, so they can begin to benefit from your increased wisdom for sharing unconditional love & nurturing friendship by killing any unresolved pain & suffering in your life that may be diminishing your ability to love them.

### My Son Wil's Wisdom for Forgiving the Unresolved Pain & Suffering in His Life

"The pain and suffering that I've accumulated throughout my life forms a barrier that prevents me from being my true self. This pain and suffering is stored in my unfair memories. These unfair memories have been created throughout my life whenever I've felt I've been treated unfairly. In order to be able to be my true self, more often, I need to learn to kill the pain and suffering in my unfair memories and remove their power over me.

My pain and suffering is triggered whenever I feel I've been treated unfairly in my adult life. When I'm treated unfairly, my negative feelings are magnified because I'm not just feeling the pain and suffering caused by the present situation but I'm also reliving the pain and suffering from all the associated unfair memories from my past.

Experiencing this avalanche of unfairness may cause me to become a different person. The anger I've accumulated in my past can come out in the present and cause me to overreact. The person I become when my emotions overwhelm me, can be angry and can treat those around me unfairly. This anger can be hard to control because it has the power of the past behind it. By learning to kill the pain and suffering in my unfair memories, I can make sure that I don't hurt the ones I love unnecessarily.

It's important that I learn to kill my feelings of unfairness so that I can limit the amount when I treat my loved ones unfairly. Whenever I'm unfair to those I love, I add to their unfair memories. By doing this, I'm inflicting my feelings of unfairness on them and passing on my anger. By controlling my own feelings I can avoid perpetuating the cycle of unfairness in others.

At times, I am unaware of how powerful my feelings of unfairness are. Since they dwell in my subconscious mind, and only surface into my conscious mind when triggered, my feelings of unfairness can hide, affect me subtly, and explode when triggered. I may also be unaware when they take control of me and cause me to treat someone unfairly. Only through reflection can I know the full impact I have on others.

If I remain unaware of the ability of my unfair memories to control me, I can live through a cycle of abuse, where I take out my anger on others without realizing the impact of my actions, and feeling my actions are justified. I need to be aware of how I act and why I act the way I do to prevent myself from hurting the ones I love. Life can be stressful and this stress can be tiring. When I'm tired I have less control over my feelings and am more prone to acting out. I have to be careful when I'm stressed and tired that I don't take it out on those that are closest to me. I also have to understand that when someone I love takes their stress out on me, it's just because they're allowing their unfair memories to control them.

Loss of love in relationships can be caused by the failure to understand the cycle of unfairness. When I take my stress out on someone, treat them unfairly, and create an unfair memory for them, I'm building the feeling of unfairness between us. When they respond by treating me unfairly in return, the cycle is perpetuated. If we aren't mindful of what we're doing, we'll strengthen the unfairness between us to the point where it pushes away the love in our relationship. This is why couples lose love for each other over time. They don't realize that they're building a wall of unfairness between them that blocks the love.

I don't have to be angry to cause someone to feel unfairly treated. I can also trigger a feeling of unfairness when I disappoint them. If I disappoint someone I love over many years, then the feelings of disappointment I create in them will build up to the point where the disappointment can block them from loving me. I have to be aware of how not only my actions, but also my inaction, can cause pain in my loved ones and limit their ability to love me.

I can help my loved ones love me with greater passion by helping them to understand the wisdom of how feelings of unfairness can control us. I can help my loved ones understand how unfair memories can cause them to not only be angry but disappointed or indifferent as well. By helping them to understand how to kill their pain and suffering, I can help them let go of their resentment, and increase their desire to share love with me and reduce their desire to share their unresolved pain and suffering with me.

The key to killing the pain and suffering in my unfair memories is to use forgiveness. Whenever I feel unfairly treated I need to forgive the person who is treating me unfairly. I also need to continually forgive all the people who have treated me unfairly in the past, especially the ones who do not deserve forgiveness. This is because being treated unfairly in the present will trigger my unfair memories of the past to generate unresolved pain and suffering from my past into my present life.

My mind in the present will wander to my past memories, and when it does, I need to practice forgiveness with each of my unfair memories and the people involved. Doing so will remove the power my unfair memories have over me in the present and diminish their power over me in the future.

By practicing forgiveness I remove the pain and suffering stored in unfair memories. As a little more of the negative energy in my unfair memories is released each time they come up and I practice forgiveness, the power of my unfair memories diminishes over time.

Eventually, the energy storehouse for my unfair memories will be empty of stress, pain and anger, and I can move on from the past and practice forgiveness in the present to prevent me from holding on to new unfair memories moving forward.

We all carry a bag of unresolved pain and suffering around with us. This bag is filled with all of the unfair memories that we haven't dealt with or are still in the process of dealing with. I've been carrying around my bag since I was a child and adding to it throughout my life. The weight of my bag is preventing me from being my true self because the pain and suffering inside of it is blocking the love I have to give from taking priority.

The time has come for me to empty my bag by practicing forgiveness. The process may take the rest of my life but by dedicating myself to practicing forgiveness I am diminishing the power of my unfair memories over time and increasing my ability to love everyone and everything in my life with great passion.

In order to forgive I am letting go of my need for revenge, justice and compensation. I believe that life isn't fair in any given instance but life is fair in the whole. I have been treated unfairly in the past and will be treated unfairly in the future. Every time I'm treated unfairly these unfair feelings motivate me to make the situation fair by getting the person that treated me unfairly to pay. This payment may satisfy my desire for revenge, justice or compensation but payment isn't always possible. Bad people sometimes get away with being bad. They don't always have to pay for what they've done. At least not every time they do something wrong. However, these bad people will get what's coming to them. Life is fair in the whole. But it may not be me who corrects the unfairness of the bad people who do me wrong. And good people can also treat me unfairly.

When others treat me unfairly, I am forgiving them even when they do not deserve forgiveness. Carrying around the pain and suffering they cause me won't hurt them, won't allow me to take revenge, won't cause justice to be done, and won't make them pay me back. All the effort I spend carrying around the pain and suffering they caused me generates more pain and suffering in my present life whenever I relive one of these painful memories, as my memories push this old pain and suffering back into my present life. So I am forgiving those that don't deserve it so that I can be free of the old pain and suffering that they caused me.

I am also sharing the wisdom I am learning with my loved ones. Even though my loved ones may continue to treat me unfairly, I continue to forgive them and I try to help them to realize what they're doing and why they're doing it, by helping them to understand why their negative emotions sometimes take control of their minds and motivate them to treat me unfairly.

And I am helping my loved ones to practice forgiveness so that they can empty their bag of unresolved pain and suffering they are carrying around with them. I am doing this because I love them and I am helping them to stop their unfair painful memories from controlling them so they can free themselves of their unresolved pain and suffering from their past.

By teaching, helping, and being patient I am working with my loved ones to break the cycle of unfairness on both sides. As my loved ones and I work on practicing this wisdom together, we are helping each other remove the blockages to our love.

The reward for practicing this wisdom is my increased capacity to feel and share continuous love, peace, joy, and compassion. By unloading my bag of unresolved pain and suffering I'm removing the weight that slows me down in life. My work may never be completely done, but the more I free myself from the unfairness in my past life, the more I am able to love in the present moment and in my future life."

End of My Son Wil's wisdom for increasing the love & forgiveness in his life by emptying his bag of unresolved pain & suffering that he has been carrying around with him in his adult life.

As his father, I am also determined to find creative ways to empty my bag of unresolved pain & suffering by practicing the nine steps to emotional freedom, whenever new unfair experiences enter my life and start to fill my bag with unresolved pain & suffering.

Fortunately, the reward for learning and then practicing the wisdom of forgiveness is the **continuous** love, peace, joy & compassion that enters our future adult lives, after we use forgiveness to kill the major unresolved pain & suffering that is still living inside our old unfair memories and that is still blocking the internal pathway to our childhood source of powerful unconditional love & forgiveness."

(Quote from the Forgiving Others Who Do Not Deserve Forgiveness section in Chapter 3 of Our Book One)

To practice asking your mind for help whenever you practice The Nine Steps to Emotional Freedom from unresolved pain & suffering, please remember when someone hurt you when you were a teenager:

**Visualizing Myself as a Teenager**

"Please visualize yourself when you were a teenager and choose a memory of unfair pain & suffering when a friend, who you trusted, betrayed you. This should be a memory of someone you have not forgiven for creating unfair pain in your teenage life.

And please use this painful memory to learn how to practice killing all the unfair pain in the memories that you may be reliving each day of your adult life.

Start by reviewing the first five steps of The Nine Steps to Emotional Freedom section in Chapter 13 of Our Book One, until you intellectually understand how these steps work and why they should work for you. They are:

Practicing Detachment
Practicing Friendship
Controlling My Mind
Practicing Fairness
Practicing Forgiveness

Now, please trigger the unfair memory from your teenage life, so you can practice these steps and prove to yourself that this wisdom will work to kill the pain that is buried inside this unfair memory.

First, say the name of the teenager who treated you unfairly. This should trigger the unfair teenage memory to start generating new pain from this unfair experience into your conscious adult mind.

Now, start practicing detachment to enable you to look at the new pain from outside of it, instead of getting lost inside the pain.

Then, start practicing controlling your mind so you can use meditation & mindfulness to calm your mind and help prevent you from mentally running away from this new pain. Just watch the pain and feel all of it. Do not try to control the pain. Just wait & watch until the pain runs out of energy and starts to disappear from your mind.

Now, when the intensity of pain has decreased, start practicing friendship by making the pain your new friend, so it can help you understand why your teenage friend treated you unfairly. And ask yourself questions, such as,

Did I contribute to my friend treating me unfairly by saying something or doing something that my friend did not like?

Now, start practicing fairness by **not** telling yourself that life is being unfair as you relive this memory, as you begin to suffer the old pain from this memory.

If you tell your memory that life is being unfair to you as you relive this teenage memory, your old memory will use the new unfair thinking energy that you have just created in your mind, to generate more pain inside your conscious mind.

Then, start practicing forgiveness by visualizing an image of your teenage friend inside your conscious mind, as you imagine forgiving your friend.

Now, imagine telling your unfair memory that you are willing to live with this unfairness and that you have forgiven your teenage friend for treating you unfairly, so there is no longer any need for the memory to generate any new pain inside your conscious mind in the future, to warn you that your teenage friend may create new unfairness in your life, whenever you relive this unfair memory again in the future because your teenage friend will not treat you unfairly again in the future.

Old unfair memories will not change their self-programmed reaction when I trigger them to generate new pain into my life, until I reprogram them with forgiveness by telling them that I can live with the unfairness because the person who hurt me unfairly in the past will not hurt me again in the future **or** by reprogramming them with the truth, such as by convincing a memory that it does not need to generate new pain into my mind to warn me that I am in danger of being hurt because life is now being fair to me and the potential unfairness that the memory is warning me about will not re-occur in the future, ever again.

If you cannot convince your memory to stop generating pain into your life, then think of this teenager's name, at least once a day for the next few days, to allow the memory to create new pain in your life each day, until it completely depletes its energy supplies that it has stored inside The Room of Feeling Energy inside your subconscious mind, until it has no energy left to generate any new pain into your life.

And make sure you do not think your life has suddenly become unfair to you whenever you relive this now painless memory again in the future because you will give this old unfair memory new thinking energy to start generating new unfair pain into your life, once again.

When you have completed the steps to kill the pain in this memory, please answer these questions:

Have I proven that the five steps to emotional freedom have worked to kill the unfair pain in this memory?

If the steps worked, why did they work?

If the steps did not work, why did they not work?

The benefits of practicing these five steps to emotional freedom are:

You will learn to forgive your friends & family members who have hurt you unfairly in the past, by first killing the unfair pain that they have created in your memories, so you will be able to generate compassion for each one of them, especially when they do not deserve your forgiveness, when you realize that you are **not** doing this to benefit them. You are doing this to stop your memories from creating new pain in your conscious mind in the future whenever you think of the names of the friends or family members who hurt you.

And you will learn to generate the courage that you require to become able to look at all the unfair painful memories that are living inside your mind and then you will realize that as you continue practicing The Wisdom to Kill the Unfairness in Your Memories, you will eventually make all the major painful memories that you may be reliving in your life each day, pain free.

Being pain free allows your internal source of love to generate increasing love, joy, peace & compassion into your life each day until it becomes continuous.

However, please be patience with your progress as you continue practicing the steps to emotional freedom during the next few months, as you kill the unresolved pain & suffering in other memories that require you to forgive yourself for the unfairness you created in someone's life or that require you to forgive someone who created unfairness in your life, as you learn to kill all the major unfair pain in your memories that may be blocking your internal connection to the unconditional love in your heart that will enable you to generate additional love, peace, joy & compassion in your adult life each day, as this connection becomes a clear & fully open pathway to your internal source of unconditional love.

Why do I lose my internal connection to unconditional love when I run away from the pain & suffering that my memories generate inside my mind? Why do I allow this to occur and how can I prevent it in the future? Q-138

Please realize that when you refuse to look inside your mind at your internal suffering, you become cut off from your connection to your internal source of unconditional love. This reduces your ability to feel increasing love, peace, joy & compassion in your adult life."

(Quote from the Visualizing Myself as a Teenager section in Chapter 23 of Our Book One)

When you are able to fully reconnect with your internal source of unconditional love, you can choose to feel continuous unconditional love in your adult life, as described by My Son Wil.

## My Son Wil's Wisdom for Choosing Continuous Unconditional Love

### The Compassionate and Loving Nature of Children

"Children are innately compassionate and loving. This is a result of their strong connection to their internal sources of unconditional love. This connection is strong due to the proximity of their age to their birth. Young children have not as yet had enough discouraging interactions with disconnected people and insane situations to erode their faith in their wisdom. Children will eventually grow into jaded adults but as long as they remain children they continue to live joyfully.

Examples of the compassion of children are provided by Maria Montessori and Theodore Rubin. They express how the compassion that exists amongst children is remarkable. It is remarkable because it does not generally exist to the same degree among adults. In this way, children offer the example of how we all should live, regardless of age. Remembering how I was as a child is the key to reconnecting with my internal source of unconditional love. This is because that connection is still there; I've simply forgotten how to use it. Remembering how I was as a child and acting as I did then is my means of reconnection.

I cannot prove to anyone that unconditional love is the inherent state of spiritual existence for all human beings. Each individual must prove that for himself or herself. Practicing The Wisdom of Children exists to help people through that process with the goal of improving the quality of their lives and spiritual existence. This work is important because it's true. It works for me. Reconnecting with the unconditional love I felt as a child makes me happier, more motivated and more able to accomplish my goals.

I am inherently an unconditionally loving person. However I find it difficult to be my true self due to my acceptance of the false expectations the world has thrust upon me.

Reconnecting with the unconditional love I felt as a child is a simple process because it doesn't require any additional evidence beyond my early life experiences. The evidence is there and it is irrefutable. Once I accept the truth of my childhood, I can begin practicing unconditional love immediately.

## Improving the Quality of My Life

I am an unconditionally loving human being. I can choose to use my knowledge to improve the quality of my life. I do so by unconditionally loving myself and those around me.

I have an alternative choice. This choice is to go on living as I am. To do so I must ignore my ability to love unconditionally and fail to acknowledge my natural state of connectedness. I must reject the evidence that is provided by my childhood memories and refuse the benefits of an unconditionally loving life.

This, as I see it, is no choice at all.

The only challenge I must meet is to truly and continuously believe in the power of unconditional love. For this to work, I must change my mind and master my ego. I must undo the damage done to me by my interaction with spiritually disconnected people and therefore the insane world I live in. In fixing myself and helping others to fix themselves, I can contribute to repairing and changing the world as I help the world to reconnect to unconditional love and to me.

## Proving that I am an Unconditional Loving Human Being

The main theme of Practicing The Wisdom of Children is proving the truth of our inherent unconditionally loving nature to ourselves using the evidence provided by our childhood memories. Doing so requires removing all the blockages caused by patterns of egoic thinking accumulated since childhood through the interaction with spiritually disconnected individuals and situations.

This process requires that I master the wisdom of killing the unfairness in my memories so that I can reconnect with my internal source of unconditional love. Killing the unfairness in my memories is important because the unfair pain I've accumulated throughout my life has created a wall that blocks my internal connection to the unconditional love inside me by confusing, distracting and disconnecting me from my true nature.

## Killing the Unfairness in My Memories

I accumulate unfair pain in my memories whenever I'm treated unfairly and I compulsively think about the unfairness of my experience. The more I compulsively think about the unfairness of my experience, the more I give the feeling of unfairness energy. Although it may be fiction, it becomes a belief that I start treating as a fact. Although it is ultimately irrelevant, I make it out to be the biggest thing in my world. This is dangerous behavior because the unfair pain in my memories exponentially grows in power and diversity. In the future, when I relive my memories of unfairness, they sprout from my subconscious into my conscious mind, forcing me to experience extra unfair pain in addition to any unfair pain I may be feeling as a direct result of events in the present. The progressively intensifying power of unfair pain that I experience as a result of this pattern of compulsive thinking and memory retention contributes to my disconnection from my internal source of unconditional love by convincing me that life, living all around me, is not only unfair but also unfair in increasingly escalating degrees.

The belief that life, living all around me, is unfair is ultimately irrelevant and only serves to hurt me in the present moment and in the long run. I must learn to choose my feelings and my memories in order to diminish their power over my thinking and perception. This will allow me to become who I truly am, an unconditionally loving person.

My wisdom for killing the unfair pain in my memories is relatively easy. False life-diminishing thoughts are thoughts that are ultimately untrue, irrelevant and hurtful to the quality of my existence. They serve no other purpose than to present me with a challenge on my quest to fulfill my true purpose in life. Dealing with them is simple. I catch and identify them in their moment of arising: the moment in which they sprout into my conscious mind. I then choose not to compulsively think about them. Thus, I refuse to feed them power. I acknowledge their existence and seek to understand them while realizing they are not who I am, how I have to be or how I have to feel. They present me with an option to feel negatively that I refuse. I remind myself that I am worthy of living and capable of success. I know that I can reprogram my memories in order to remove their mastery of me. I allow my false life-diminishing thoughts to arise and then subside back into my subconscious without compulsively thinking of them. Starved of attention, my false life-diminishing thoughts, and the unfair pain associated with them, lose their power in the present moment and in the long term. Over time, the unfair pain in my memories diminishes. The wall blocking my connection to my internal source of unconditional love is eroded. As a result, I become more and more the person I am meant to be.

In this way, I master the mechanic of my memory. Memories are packets of emotion, both negative and positive, that are associated with my past life experiences. Memories are the vehicles through which my unfair pain is stored and the mechanism through which past emotions sprout into my mind.

When my memories contain positive emotions I can be tempted to compulsively think about the acquisition of pleasurable experiences. This compulsive thinking distracts me from my true purpose in life and leads me to indulge in pleasurable experiences for the sake of pleasure, no matter how detrimental they may be to me in the present moment and in the long run. This is the source of my addictions. I obsessively indulge in activities I enjoy to the exclusion of accomplishing my goals because those goals require work to attain. When the positive emotions released by my memories convince me to compulsively think about the pleasurable experiences I'm having and cause me to work towards perpetuating them, I must remember that this pleasure is in large part a false alternative to my true existence.

Pleasure in itself is a worthy reward and a worthwhile experience. However, false pleasure in excess of that to be found in the present moment is to be avoided because it serves as a mental distraction from my true existence. Ultimately, pleasure derived from material experience pales in comparison to the pleasure that I feel as a result of my internal connection to unconditional love. Thus, I must control how much I indulge in material pleasure, ensuring that I'm not led to compulsive thinking by the emotions stored within my memories, and making sure that my enjoyment of material pleasure never blocks my connection to my internal source of unconditional love. I must truly enjoy, not falsely indulge.

When my memories contain negative emotions I can feel as if the world is being disproportionately unfair to me and this feeling can cause me to lose my motivation. When a negative memory sprouts into my conscious mind, I have the choice of whether to feed it energy or not. By choosing not to feed it energy, choosing not to compulsively think about the negative thoughts and emotions that it contains, I am able to diminish its power over me. I realize that negative emotions and thoughts contained within my memories are irrelevant. My memory of being treated unfairly in the past is irrelevant to the present moment. While I may be in the process of being treated unfairly in the present moment, I remember that in the grand scheme of things, life is fair and this too shall pass. I'm never in danger of being hurt, not truly. The magnificence of My Soul and its connection to unconditional love is untouchable and always available to me if I choose to connect with it. That's all I ever need in life to be happy, joyous and secure. The only things that can hurt me are my worries.

It is important for me to remember that I am not my feelings. I am not my mind either. I am the compassionate watcher that exists before thought. I am who I truly am when I'm not thinking. This primacy means that I have control over what I think about and how I feel. Life is entirely experiential. It flows through the filter of perception. Nothing exists for me divorced from how I perceive it. Thus, I can control my existence, make it pure, by controlling how I think so I can choose how I feel. This is free will.

## Using My Free Will to Choose My Feelings

Free will allows me to decide between being either inside or outside my unfair pain. I can be lost inside my unfair pain. I can compulsively think about it and let it consume me. Or I can exist outside my unfair pain and realize that it needn't define who I am, that it needn't consume me. I can look back at the unfair experience that is the source of my unfair pain and realize that it is over and ultimately irrelevant to the present moment. I can use my free will to free myself from the burden of the hurt of my past. I stop feeding my unfair memories and they lose their power. I stop them from hurting me now and in the future.

Stress and worry are caused by disproportional, inappropriate and inaccurate thoughts and emotions. The past is impossible to change and the future has yet to happen. All that exists is the present moment. Thus, thoughts and emotions should be tailored in size and shape to appropriately suit the demands of the present moment. How much energy does this task need to get done? How should I feel about this task truly?

In my process of self-discovery, I must realize that the challenges presented by my mind are my friends. The unfair pain in my memories provides me with learning opportunities and the opportunity to grow and excel spiritually. Perfection is boring because upon its attainment, there's nothing left to do. Every story needs a hero and every hero needs a flaw. Flaws exist to be improved upon and improvements provide the arc of the story. If there is no deficiency, there can be no goal. So I welcome the unfair pain in my memories, my false life-diminishing thoughts and my memories as companions and friends on my journey of spiritual discovery.

Exercising understanding, self-discipline and mindfulness allows me to attain my goal of living a meditative life characterized by my connection to my internal source of unconditional love. The energy supplies that are present in The Storage Room of Feeling Energy for my false life-diminishing thoughts and unfair memories will eventually be exhausted. I am gaining a better understanding of my mind, how it works, the dangers it presents and most importantly the potential that it offers.

Throughout my journey it's important not to judge myself, my thoughts or my emotions. They are ultimately all neutral in nature. They are only positive or negative when I project those qualities upon them. Decision making leads to more thinking, often negative, that I must avoid. I must only concern myself with the demands of the present moment, for that is all that truly exists, and then focus on being the best I can be in the now.

I can find the truth behind my memories by reflecting upon them. My false life-diminishing thoughts and unfair memories often spout into my conscious mind incomplete and inaccurate. The unfair pain in my memories exists to intensify my pain now and in the future. It seeks to grow its strength, perpetuating itself and increasing its power over me. This process, as it is in any competition, is more about winning than it is about fair and balanced play. My unfair pain is by definition unfair. It fights dirty and is unconcerned about its legitimacy. Knowing this, I can reflect on the unfair experience that originally caused my unfair pain and realize that it wasn't nearly as unfair as my memory makes it out to be. I also remember that anything that happened in the past is ultimately irrelevant in any case. Seeking accuracy in my remembrance leads me to replace my disproportionately unfair memories with true memories to which I can feel a vastly diminished feeling of unfairness.

**Practicing Forgiveness**

Mastering the unfair pain in my memories ends with me practicing forgiveness. I forgive when I consciously decide to excuse or pardon someone for treating me unfairly. By forgiving someone, I dismiss any desire for revenge or demands for justice. I relieve myself of the burden of pain, guilt and obligation associated with being taken advantage of and putting myself in a position to be victimized. I remove my need to exact retribution.

Forgiveness is ultimately superior to vengeance because of the primacy of the present moment, the irrelevancy of the past and the necessity of maintaining my connection to my internal source of unconditional love. Exercising forgiveness allows me to diminish the power of my unfair pain, false life-diminishing thoughts and memories because it prevents me from compulsively thinking about the injustice that was done to me.

To forgive others I must first forgive myself. I must forgive myself for feeling the way I do when I'm treated unfairly. I must forgive myself for the way I may act in the heat of the moment, the shame I may feel at being victimized and the desire for brutal vengeance that I feel. I must understand that what happened to me was not my fault and that, ultimately, everything will be ok. Letting go of my feelings of unfairness and not judging my thoughts and emotions while understanding what they are and why they occur, enables me to free my mind of this unfairness.

Once I'm free of my personal obligations to the unfairness that I endured, I can then free others of their personal obligations to me. In most cases, revenge and the process needed to obtain it are not worth the cost of losing my connection to my internal source of unconditional love. There may be times when revenge must be obtained but it's unlikely that I will encounter such a case in my lifetime. Also, forgiving does not necessarily mean dismissing unfair actions and their perpetrators completely. Instead, forgiving myself and the others associated with the unfairness perpetrated against me is meant to prevent disproportionate reactions. Ideally, I will act appropriately and proportionately to address the demands of the present moment, divorced from its connection to the past and free of any emotional reaction. This will make me more prudent and most importantly happier. I will be free to spend more time maintaining my connection with my internal source of unconditional love.

## Practicing Thankfulness

Diminishing the unfair pain in my memories will allow me to practice thankfulness. As I connect with my internal source of unconditional love, I begin to be filled once more with joy. I begin to feel unconditional love for myself and all living things around me. I become empowered and astonished at the wonders in life. Becoming unconditionally loving works in a similar way to becoming obsessed with unfairness but with opposite results. Unconditional love begets more unconditional love and loving unconditionally empowers me to become more unconditionally loving now and in the future.

Unconditional love leads to thankfulness. I feel thankful for life because it's miraculous. I feel thankful for all living things because they are also miraculous because they have the ability to share their love for living life with me.

My unconditional love and thankfulness improves my existence and the existences of others. This is because unconditional love and thankfulness are infectious. Sharing my joy and the methods through which I attain it allow me to spread unconditional love to those around me. This is how I nurture true friendship. True connections between me and another person occur when our souls interact. This connection exists free of the thought and pretense that is the basis for thought based human interaction. The most meaningful communication between people occurs when they're not saying anything and instead completely present in the now with each other as their spiritually based unconditional love bonds them together.

## The Key to Choosing My Feelings

In conclusion, the key to happiness & success in life is managing my thoughts and emotions through continuous meditation.

Meditation is practicing Mindfulness to maintain my connection to the continuous present moment, which enables me to feel continuous love, peace, joy & compassion from all the life in the universe.

I am meditating continually with the goal of maintaining perpetual mindfulness.

Doing so allows me to exist as I truly am. Everything else, all the techniques that I will learn, all the understanding I will gain, all relates back to this central goal. I'm removing the obstacles, such as killing the unfair pain in my memories, that are preventing me from regaining mindfulness and I am learning to use the tools necessary to maintain mindfulness.

**Living Spiritually and Mindfully**

Living spiritually means living mindfully to enable me to fully connect to my internal source of unconditional love, to enable my unconditional love to supply me with continuous peace and joy, plus powerful motivation, to help me fulfill my purpose in life.

Living Mindfully is knowing what is happening inside my mind in the present moment, while it is happening, no matter what it is, to become able to spot any new distractions that may enter my mind, to enable me to manage my distractions by preventing them from gaining control of my mind and actions.

All I need to do is regain mindfulness whenever I lose it and then practice maintaining continuous mindfulness, to enable me to manage all my feelings and to prevent me from being distracted, as I work on my goals to fulfill my life's purpose."

(Selected Quotations from My Son Wil's Wisdom for Choosing His Feelings section in Chapter 26 of our Book One)

**Reaching My Full Potential**

"I am beginning to realize that our lives as human beings on Our Precious Mother Earth reach their full potential when we share our unconditional love & we nurture true friendship with all human beings, as we savor sharing their love for all life, especially their love for us, as we become their spiritual brothers & sisters.

I feel grateful for my gift of being born with the ability to share unconditional love & nurture true friendship, as I say, "Thank You" to my friends & family for sharing their love with me, as I share my love with them, as I experience becoming who I was born to be, as I choose to be an unconditionally loving human being, each moment of every day of my future adult life.

Our ancient sages have tried to convince us to practice the wisdom for sharing unconditional love. This ancient wisdom is contained in the memories of the unconditional love of our childhood, when we felt our love **for** all life and when we felt the love **from** all life, growing inside us. This ancient wisdom benefits us, as adults, when we remember experiencing the unconditional love & the desire for true friendship during our childhood.

To help you to relive these childhood memories, it is important to learn the wisdom in Our Book One that will give you the tools to understand how your mind works, to make it easier to relive the unconditional love of your childhood. These memories are important for you to experience, so you can prove that you were born as an unconditionally loving human being. Then, upon this proof of your childhood wisdom that helped you to unconditional love all life when you were a child, you can start to add the wisdom in Our Book Two to your adult life, to increase the love, peace, joy & compassion that you now share with your friends & family, as you begin to realize that you have not lost your childhood ability to feel an immense passion for living and a compelling desire to share new fun & adventures with your friends & family, as you learn to live as a child again, as you start to re-experience the intense unconditional love that you felt as a child, as you remember that this love continuously supplied you with abundant passion for enjoying your life and with powerful motivation to fill each day of your childhood with new fun & adventures.

One of the major tools available for you to use to facilitate this process of increasing the passion in your adult life is "Rewriting The Wisdom of Children In Your Own Words" about how the wisdom is able to bring increasing love, peace, joy & compassion into your adult life, as you practice The Wisdom of Children each day. Writing about your experiences in your own words will make it easier for you to explain this wisdom to your friends & family, when they ask you why you are a happier human being who has a renewed passion for sharing fun & adventures with them.

May your love, peace, joy & compassion increase each day of your future life, as you work hard to achieve the objective stated at the beginning of the Sharing Love & Adventures with Friends & Family section in Chapter 2 of Our Book One, that says,

"Our Book is a Self Help Guide for all adult human beings who desire to live in a state of **continuous** love, peace, joy & compassion, as they share unconditional love & nurture true friendship with their friends & family."

And if you have already achieved the state of experiencing continuous love, peace, joy & compassion each day of your adult life, then I congratulate you, for you are indeed a rare & precious human being.

Unfortunately for many of us, it is a long & difficult path to navigate, to become able to choose our feelings, so we can kill all the major unfair pain in our memories, so that we can become able to achieve the state of **continuous** love, peace, joy & compassion. And if you are a slow learner of this wisdom, like me, "Do not Ever Give Up" trying to use the power of this wisdom, as you work hard to implement this wisdom into your daily life, because it is worth all the hard work that it may take, to prove to yourself that you are a rare & precious unconditionally loving human being who is reaching your full potential, as you begin living in a state of continuous love, peace, joy & compassion, and as you share unconditional love & nurture true friendship with all human beings, especially your friends & family."

(Modified Quotes from the Reaching My Full Potential section in Chapter 27 of Our Book One)

## Thank You for Embracing the Love in Your Heart

"Thank you for embracing the unconditional love in your heart to become able to increase the joy & happiness that you share with your friends, your family & the world, which includes me who is a member of your spiritual family.

I hope & pray The Wisdom of Children described in Our Books One & Two will continue to help you, as it is continuing to help My Son & me, to fully reconnect to your childhood ability to share continuous unconditional love & nurture continuous true friendship with your friends, family & all the life that surrounds you.

Please learn to become a Master of Meditation, Mindfulness & How to Control the Fairness in Your Mind, so you will become able to forgive those members of your friends & family who have hurt you unfairly over the years, so you will become able to start loving them unconditionally once again, as you were able to do as a young child, with every human being that you met in your childhood, as you offered each one an opportunity to share unconditional love & nurture true friendship with you.

Your challenge as an adult is to fully re-learn The Wisdom of Children that you intuitively understood and experienced as a young child, so you can forgive those who have hurt you unfairly, especially those who do not deserve your love because of their bad behavior.

This may not be an easy challenge for you, when you decide to accept this challenge. If you do not accept this challenge you will continue to carry around unresolved unfair pain & suffering that you will continue to feel whenever you relive one of your unfair memories. After you forgive the person who created this unfairness in your memory, the unresolved pain & suffering will disappear forever. The choice to forgive is completely yours to make, but it may not be easy for you to forgive. Forgiveness sometimes takes a long time to accomplish. Please remember that you are not doing this to benefit those who hurt you unfairly in the past. You are doing this to stop your memories from creating new unresolved pain & suffering in your life in the future.

This is why it may take you months or years to forgive not just one person, but all those who have hurt you unfairly over the years. How long it takes will depend on how much unresolved pain & suffering you have stored in your memories of the unfair experiences in your life, as you grew from a young child into the adult you are today, experiences that have created unfair memories that continue to generate unresolved pain & suffering in your life whenever you relive one of these unfair memories. You need to learn how to kill each memory's ability to generate new pain & suffering into your life, pain & suffering that may be blocking your access to your internal source of unconditional love, before you can fully reconnect to your childhood ability to share **continuous** unconditional love & nurture continuous true friendship with those you love, today.

When you start this challenge you will begin to experience reduced unfair pain & suffering and increasing love, peace, joy & compassion in your daily life within the first month of practicing this wisdom. This positive result of embracing The Wisdom of Children will help motivate you to continue learning more of the wisdom in Our Books, to enable you to increase the amount of unconditional love that you experience each day and then share with your friends & family, as a result of applying The Wisdom of Children to your life.

I know this is true because My Son & I experience increasing unconditional love, peace, joy & compassion in our daily lives as we continue to practice The Wisdom of Children.

Please generate the courage that you need inside you, to become able to look at your painful memories, so you can start killing the unresolved pain & suffering that is buried inside them, so they will lose their ability to hurt you in the future, to enable you to start increasing the amount of unconditional love, peace, joy &

compassion that you are able to experience each day of your future life.

My Son and I will continue to help you to practice this wisdom, as you become a Master of Meditation, Mindfulness & How to Control the Fairness in Your Mind, to enable you to learn to choose more of your life-enhancing feelings, instead of allowing the unresolved pain & suffering to continue living inside your conscious mind, by providing you with additional wisdom that will help you to improve your ability to share unconditional love & nurture true friendship with your friends & family."

(Modified quote from the Thank You for Embracing the Love in Your Heart section in Chapter 28 of Our Book One)

**The Wisdom of My Perfection Makes Me Worthy of Living**

"I am perfect because I was born this way, with the perfect ability to love all the life that is surrounding me and to feel the reciprocal love from all this life, as it nourishes me, as I wonder how it was created, as I enjoy its beauty, and as its desire to live & thrive, fills me with its powerful passion for living and encourages me to seek out new life giving fun & adventures with my friends & family, as this passion makes me feel worthy of living, as it flows through me into my life experiences.[72]

I am choosing to embrace these life-enhancing feelings and I allow them to blossom in my heart, as I learn to detach from any unresolved pain & suffering that may enter my conscious mind, as I share the unconditional love, beauty & passion for living that I am continuing to receive from all the life surrounding me.

This ability to share love enables me to love my friends & family and to forgive them when they hurt me unfairly and it makes me worthy of living my unique & blessed life as an unconditional loving human being on Our Precious Mother Earth.

This loving energy from all the life in the universe flows through all living things and that is why I am blessed as this love energy flows through me and encourages me to work on My Goals for Today. This happens automatically, as long as I am able to stop any fear, anger, worry or stress that enters my conscious mind and tries to block my pathway to this energy of life, which is the love energy that is continuously flowing into my conscious mind from My Internal Source of Unconditional Love.

To be able to do this, I have decided to practice The Wisdom of Children to pay the price required to replace the fear, anger, worry or stress that may enter my mind in the future, with continuous love, peace, joy & compassion by using this wisdom to keep the pathway to My Internal Source of Unconditional Love fully open & clear of obstacles that will start to close down this pathway, when I allow negative unfair feelings to take control of my conscious mind.

A clear pathway to this love energy enables me to accomplish my primary goal for today which is to share continuous unconditional love & to nurture true friendship, a goal which may be delayed, whenever I start to relive the fear, anger, worry or stress that starts to creates despair in my life, whenever my unfair memories or my ego begin to generate painful feelings inside me, as they start to block the pathway to my internal source of love, as they begin to diminish my motivation to continue working on my goals, unless I practice killing these unfair painful feelings quickly to clear my pathway to the full power of the love energy in my internal source of unconditional love.

As this new day of my future life begins, the universal love that I am receiving from all the life around me is encouraging me to share unconditional love & true friendship with friends & family and others who I will meet today, even if the opportunity to share our passion for living will last for only for a few moments, as I continue to ask myself these questions during this new day of my life.

How will I nurture true friendship with each person that I meet today? Q-152

How will I practice the Nine Steps to Emotional Freedom to enable me to kill any new feelings of pain & suffering that may enter my life today? Q-153

How will I practice controlling my thinking energy so I can stay fully connected to my internal source of love today, to enable me to greet those I meet today with abundant feelings of love that they will feel when they look into my eyes? Q-154"

(Quote from The Wisdom of My Perfection Makes Me Worthy of Living section in Chapter 29 of Our Book One)

**Using My Perfection to Help Others become Perfect**

"The Wisdom of Children is composed of a mental & physical practice. The mental practice is the nurturing & protecting of the love, peace, joy & compassion that lives inside me and the physical practice of sharing this unconditional love when I offer true friendship to another human being."

(Quote from The Essence of The Wisdom of Children section in Chapter 8 of Our Book One)

"Once this wisdom starts to benefit you, you will begin to help your friends & family to bring more joy into their lives, just by becoming a more loving & compassionate human being who exhibits an increasing desire to share unconditional love & nurture true friendship.

And please forgive us for the repetitive nature of the questions. We have asked you similar questions, in slightly different ways throughout Our Books One & Two, to help you to obtain a clearer & more precise understanding of this wisdom, as your daily practice of this wisdom increases, as your mind makes this wisdom into a belief structure that your mind automatically uses to understand why other human beings treat you fairly or unfairly in your future life, when they try to share joy or pain with you and when they accept or reject your offers of love & understanding.

This process of increasing the passion for living that I share with other human beings is made possible by my daily practice of The Wisdom of Children as it helps me to understand the new feelings that I experience each day and also helps me to understand & respect the privacy of the feelings of my friends & family, as I wait for them to share their thoughts & feelings with me, as I allow them to live their lives with me or without me, but also without my advice, if possible, unless they ask for help & advice when they share their thoughts & feelings with me as I endeavor to love & respect them unconditionally, continuously & forever.

Knowing that my friends & family are trying to live their lives as unconditional loving human beings and are also trying to share true friendship with those they love, is what is important to me, even if I may be unable to share my life with them, at this time. But then again, who knows what may happen in the future as our mutual love motivates us to be together, as one big family who shares hopes & dreams and then works together to make some of those dreams become a reality.

And hopefully in the future, I will become able to share more of my life with those I love, as my desire for a fun filled future life continues to inspire me and as I realize that our ultimate human destiny is to be together, loving one another in this life & the next, as I cherish my future vision of all human beings on Our Precious Mother Earth coming together in mutual self-interest as we; help one another, love each other, support one another, and of course forgive each other, especially when those who hurt us do not deserve our forgiveness or when we hurt ourselves & others when our plans for a better life go awry.

Then, as we try to live peacefully together once again, as our mutual love for all life starts to heal the wounds of our failures & disappointments, as best it can, hopefully we will realize that sharing unconditional love & nurturing true friendship is what all human beings are born to do.

I can prove this is true in my own life, by looking back at the memories of my childhood when I felt love for everyone & when I felt loved by all the life in the universe, and by looking at my friends & family as my desire to share love & friendship with them continues to grow."

(Quote from the Using My Perfection to Help Others become Perfect section in Chapter 30 of Our Book One)

## Overview of the Wisdom in Our Book Series

"The four books in The Wisdom of Children series help us to increase the Love, Peace, Joy & Compassion in Our Lives until it becomes continuous.

Our Book One "Learning to Understand My True Self" helps us to increase the love, peace, joy & compassion in our daily lives by teaching us how to kill the unresolved pain & suffering that is buried in our old unfair memories that many of us keep reliving each day of our lives, as we try to fully reconnect to the Internal Source of Unconditional Love of our childhood that we were born possessing and that many of us have diminished or lost, to enable us to experience the continuous love, peace, joy & compassion that we remember experiencing when we were children.

My Son & I will help you to understand The Wisdom of Children which helps us to fully reconnect to this continuous love, peace, joy & compassion and we will help you to realize the benefits of practicing this wisdom as we tell you stories of how we successfully applied this wisdom to our lives to increase the unconditional love that we share with our friends & family.

Our Book Two "Understanding How My Mind Works" helps us to learn meditation & mindfulness techniques to enable us to understand how our minds actually work and to enable us to understand how our minds should work, to help us correct the errors in our thinking, as we use our reasoning ability to control our thinking energy that we use to power our motivation to accomplish the goals for our lives.

Our Book Three "Learning to Choose My Feelings" helps us to practice choosing all our feelings, especially the feelings that nurture & protect our continuous love, peace, joy & compassion, as we learn to kill the control that our Egos have over our lives, as we stop our bad habits & our procrastinating that diminish our opportunities for increasing the life-enhancing feelings that nurture happiness & success in our future lives.

Our Book Four "Increasing My Love for All Life" helps us to learn how to maximize the love, peace, joy & compassion in our lives by helping us to learn how to embrace & forgive those who hurt us, so we can remove all the pain in our hearts that prevents us from fully loving our friends & family, once again, as we learn to pass on our wisdom for increasing the happiness & success in our lives, to our children & our grandchildren, by learning to understand what is motivating them as they grow up, so we can help them to live in continuous joy & happiness and not make the same mistakes that we made when we were young, because we did not know how to protect our childhood ability to fully love & fully forgive our friends & family.

Unfortunately, many of us diminished or lost our childhood ability to love our life when our passion started to hide under all the memories of the unresolved pain & suffering that we experienced growing up.

In summary, the wisdom in Our Books helps us to kill all the major unresolved pain & suffering that is buried inside our painful memories and to kill the errors in our thinking, to enable us to fully reconnect to The Internal Source of Unconditional Love of our childhood that we were born possessing. This reconnection enables us to feel an increasing love for all life, especially for our friends & family and to feel loved by all the life that surrounds us, an ability that we possessed when we were young. As children we felt intense love for our friends & family until we were treated unfairly, at times, and we did not know how to stop this unfair pain from hurting us, when our offers of love & friendship were rejected by the neurotic people in our childhood, who were unable to accept our love and who treated us unfairly by lying to us, manipulating us, stealing from us, or abusing us.

Fortunately, The Wisdom of Children helps us to understand how this unresolved pain & suffering is generated inside our minds when we relive these unfair memories and this wisdom helps us to kill this old pain & suffering, so we can replace it with feelings of continuous love, peace, joy & compassion that motivate us to share new adult fun & adventures with our friends & family. Please ask yourself these questions,

Is it possible to believe that The Wisdom of Children may help me to increase the joy & happiness in my adult life? Why? Q-11

How does The Wisdom of Children become a belief structure that anchors itself to my real childhood ability to unconditionally love all the life around me and to my adult ability to love my friends & family?

"Belief structures create a filter through which the chaos of our external perceptions about life are sifted into a mental reality that becomes a stable & loving presence inside our human minds." (Modified quote from Frank Herbert's Dune series)

"Our belief structures help us to realize that we are not just our bodies, as we try to understand the feelings, thoughts & images that enter our minds from the outside world, as they live with us for a while and then disappear from our minds each day. They help us to define who we are as human beings, as our Free Will helps us to use these feelings, thoughts & images to create our mental perceptions of the real world that exists outside our minds & bodies.

As this is happening, there still remains inside our minds, a quiet sanctuary that is free of the feelings, thoughts & images of the outside world, a sanctuary where we can go and where nothing lives except the knowledge we were given when we were born, that each of us is an eternal spiritual being who is loved by all creation, as we wait for our feelings, thoughts & images to help us define who we are as spiritual beings living inside human bodies on Our Precious Mother Earth.

Only when we realize that this innate knowledge is true, can we begin to understand why we were born with a powerful desire to love everyone in our lives, as we try to fully reconnect to this universal love of our childhood in our adult lives and as we try to forgive those in the outside world who do not deserve our forgiveness."

(Modified quote from the Overview of the Wisdom in Our Book Series section in Chapter 5 of Our Book One)

End of the Introduction section of Our Book Two which includes an overview of the wisdom in Our Book One which will help the reader to fully benefit from the wisdom in Our Book Two.

# Table of Contents

# Disclaimer

Our Book Two of The Wisdom of Children Series of Books contains our understanding of the wisdom of the authors who we have referred to in the contents of our book, referenced in the bibliography and recommended in the readings list, and does not necessarily reflect the views of these authors, since our understanding is only our interpretation of the wisdom contained in the authors' books, videos & other teachings.

Our Books One & Two describe how my mind & my son's mind works. We have made the assumption that all human minds work using the same principles that we describe in our book. Only you, the reader, will be able to determine if this assumption is true or not true by looking inside your mind and comparing what you find there to our description of how our human minds work, as we describe how our minds process the pain & joy in our lives, from the time we are born until we reach adulthood, and then into future, as we describe the challenges that we face as we endeavor to share continuous love, peace, joy & compassion with our friends & family in our adult lives.

The publication of Our Books Three & Four of the Practicing The Wisdom of Children series depends on my continuing good health as I complete the final drafts of these books and may also depend on other unknown circumstances. There is no guarantee these books will be published but My Son & I will do our best to publish them, so our readers may enjoy them and then share the wisdom in these books with their friends & family.

The US spelling of "practicing" is used in Our Books instead of the British spelling of "practising" which has the same meaning as the US version when used as a verb.

# Dedication to Byron Katie

My mentor & role model who taught me how my mind should work.

(Please refer to the Obtaining Help from Byron Katie section in Chapter 1 of Our Book Two)

# Chapter 1

## My Image of the World that I Create in My Mind

When my mind processes a particular sense impression, such as seeing an object, my other senses for smelling, hearing, touching & tasting shut down until the process of seeing is complete. Then I smell, then I hear, then I touch & then I taste. They happen one after another, very quickly.

The first contact I have with the world is through my five senses which are non-conceptual. When I look at a person, I have the opportunity to see the whole person. The moment the perceptual image of the whole person enters my mind I select only fragments of the whole image. I single out certain things and neglect the rest. For example, I may concentrate on the color of the person's eyes & their smile. Afterwards, I may say that the person has lovely blue eyes and a wonderful smile. This is what I remember. I have actually seen many aspects of the person but I only remember the aspects that stood out at the time, due to my past conditioning & my habitual way of looking at other people.

Direct perception is non-conceptual, but as soon as my conceptual mind takes over, I label whatever I perceive, adding many things & omitting many others.

Whenever I see, hear, smell, taste & touch, I create mental images about the world in my mind to which I add names, which I then evaluate as good or bad and positive or negative. These labels are the basis from which I generate my feelings of desire or aversion and love or hate. This constant process of artificially imposing names & evaluations on my perceptions has nothing to do with the qualities of the objects that I perceive.

Unfortunately, my mental creations are the source of future delusions that may occur in my life, when I misperceive the objects of my senses and attach the wrong evaluations & the wrong feelings to them.

This results in an image of the world that I have created in my mind about the events in my life that may cause me future problems when I do not correctly evaluate the feelings, thoughts & images of my perceptions, before I store them away as memory seeds in my subconscious mind for later use, when a future event in my life triggers my memory seed of a past event to sprout back into my conscious mind & my present life.

When a memory seed of a past event sprouts into my conscious mind, it brings a feeling, thought & image and an evaluation with it that may be wrong. When I follow the advice of a wrong feeling and act upon it, then I create negative consequences for my future life which are called My Negative Karma. The consequences of doing the wrong thing will come back into my life and punish me someday in the future.

So I need a method to evaluate my memory seeds when they sprout into my conscious mind, before I grasp onto a feeling, thought or image and act upon the advice contained in a memory that contains errors, to stop creating negative Karma in my future life, by not believing that the erroneous evaluations I have made in my life and stored in my memory seeds are true, and then by not treating my friends & family unfairly with these false evaluations.

When a sprouted memory seed from a past event contains a feeling & an evaluation that is true, then the advice contained in the memory seed may be beneficial to my life when I decide to follow its advice, when a similar event occurs in my future. This creates My Positive Karma which generates increasing love, peace, joy & compassion in my future life.

Unfortunately, my memories may carry incorrect evaluations of past events in my life, so I am learning to evaluate all my newly sprouted memory seeds to spot each feeling, thought & image from a memory seed that is not correct & that is harmful to my life and then I am learning to not blindly follow the advice contained in the memory seed, so I do not accept the wrong advice contained in my deluded or erroneous memory seeds, by killing these errors when I search for truth in my memories.

## Mindfulness

I search for the truth in my memories & my thinking by learning to practice Mindfulness each moment of every day of my life.

Mindfulness is knowing what is happening in my mind in the present moment, while it is happening, no matter what it is. (Modified Quote from Diamond Mind by Rob Nairn)

To be able to evaluate my thoughts, feelings, images & memories correctly, I am learning to rest in a state of Mindfulness as I hear things, see things, smell things, taste things & touch things, so I do not react in any way, so I do not grasp or attach to the wrong advice contained in an incorrect feeling, thought or image, and so I do not follow the wrong advice contained in an incorrect evaluation of a past experience that is stored in a memory seed.

To evaluate my life experiences correctly, I am learning to rest in the precision & newness of the present moment. This is the uncontrived state of being, in which I am totally uninvolved when I am not labeling or manipulating or making up names or concepts. I am just resting, conscious & alert with a clear mind, without grasping or attaching to any feeling, thought or image from my actual life experiences, or from a memory that I am observing with My Compassionate Watcher at the present time. This is the state of Mindfulness in which I am resting in the Clarity & Truth of My Mind which I experience as Resting in the Arms of God & Just Being, without indulging in any pleasant, neutral or painful desires that may be triggered by my memories or the current events in my life.

In this meditative state of Mindfulness, I am able to spot my newly sprouted memory seeds, or my new feelings, thoughts & images from My Awareness of My Connection to all the life that surrounds me, when my perceptions of this life arise in my conscious mind, as

I use the Clarity & Truth of My Mind to ask questions, so I can evaluate the truth or the mistakes contained in my new thoughts, feelings, images & memories before I decide to speak or take any action. [73]

I create Mindfulness by simply resting my mind in its own nature.[74]

I do not prolong a previous feeling, thought, image or memory.

I do not beckon the next or future feeling, thought, image or memory.

I am resting my mind in the awareness of the present moment, as I embrace the external awareness of my connection to the love emanating **from** all life in the universe and as I embrace the internal awareness of my connection to the powerful unconditional love in my heart **for** all the life that is surrounding me.

I am resting my mind by detaching from all the existing distractions in my mind that may try to start controlling my mind, as I use my Mindfulness to observe all the revealed activities of my mind.

I am resting my mind naturally & expansively without attaching to any new thoughts, feelings images or memories that may enter my mind, as I use my Mindfulness to observe all the revealed activities of my mind.

I am resting my mind in such a way that my mind becomes self-illuminating and clear in itself by using the Clarity & Truth of My Mind to prevent distortions of "What Is" when I receive perceptions through my five senses, or when I relive my memories, or when I watch my imagination describe my potential future life. [75]

Then, I am asking myself these questions as I practice using Mindfulness to live continuously in the present moment:

How do I allow my mind to rest in its own nature in a state of Mindfulness to enable me to know what is happening in my mind in the present moment, while it is happening, no matter what it is, as I watch my mind working?

Based on my understanding of how my mind works, how do I recreate the external world inside my mind?   Q-155

**Treating My Newly Sprouted Memories as Dreams**

A memory seed is a memory of an event in my life that is stored in my subconscious mind. The memory seed stores my evaluation of the event as being, beneficial, neutral or harmful to my life & well-being, and my memory seed stores my feeling about the event, such as the physical feeling of pleasure or pain and the emotional feeling of joy or dislike.

I am examining my memories for any errors about the events in my life that are stored as memories in my subconscious mind, to ensure my memories contain a true description of the events in my life. Until this examination is complete, I regard all my newly sprouted memory seeds as dreams. The feelings, thoughts & images of my dreams that are created by my newly sprouted memory seeds, when they arise into my conscious mind, are potentially not real and they may not be a true description of me, my character, my life, or my relationships with my friends & family. [76]

Why do I regard my sprouted memory seeds as if they were dreams until I can find out if they are true or untrue? Q-157

To help me decide if my dreams are true or false descriptions of the events in my life, I am asking questions to kill any errors in the feelings, thoughts & images in my mind at the present time, These questions help me to evaluate or judge what is true about the events in my life.

**Meditating to help Correct the Errors in My Thinking**

My mind processes over 60,000+ feelings, thoughts & images, each day. [77]

Many of my feelings, thoughts & images are from the memory seeds that are stored in my subconscious mind. My objective is to use meditation & mindfulness to observe my feelings, thoughts & images, so I can pick out the positive life-enhancing feelings that will help motivate me to accomplish My Goals for Today and the positive thoughts & images that will offer me new ideas that will help me to increase the peace, joy, happiness & compassion in my life, both now and in the future. Many of my feelings, thoughts & images sprout into my conscious mind and then disappear in less than a second.

**Obtaining Help from Byron Katie**

Byron Katie wrote a wonderful book called, "Loving What Is" that contains the wisdom of truth & untruth that we can use to correct the errors in our thinking. I highly recommend that you read this book to help you increase your ability to share unconditional love and nurture true friendship with those you love.

As I summarized Byron Katie's book in my own words, I began to realize that when life is being unfair to me in the present moment, when someone is being unfair to me, I may allow my mind to conclude that my future life will be unfair to me again in the future. When I start to believe that my future life will be unfair, this untrue thought will start to generate errors in my thinking when I start to believe that this unfairness will come into my future life and steal my joy & happiness away from me. We call this fear of future loss or failure by the name Primordial Fear which we will discuss in more detail in Our Book Three. When I allow primordial fear to make me afraid of future events, I become unable to accept & love what is real. And what is real, is the truth that my future life will ultimately be fair to me because the future fairness in my life is protected by The Law of Karma.

Bryon Katie helped me to realize that all that is, is reality and reality is not my dream world that I create in my mind when I start to believe that my future life will be unfair to me. And Byron helped me to correct this error in my thinking by accepting the truth that my future life will ultimately be fair to me and to my friends & family.

(Please refer to the Overview of The Buddhist Law of Karma section in Chapter 23 of Our Book One)

As I read Byron's book, I helped to capture the power of Byron Katie's wisdom that I wanted to apply to my life, by changing the word "you" to "I" to change her words into the first person singular, so the passages in her book became more personal whenever I re-read her wisdom. Making this wisdom more personal helped me to understand the immense power of Byron Katie's wisdom, as I began to think about using the power of this wisdom to bring increased love, peace, joy & compassion into my life, by helping me to kill the errors in my thinking that may generate future pain & suffering in my life whenever I start believing that my future life will become unfair to me. The rest of Byron Katie's words & phraseology I have left largely intact, to retain the flavor of Byron Katie's writing as she offered me her wisdom, as I read her book and summarized its wisdom in my own words.

As you read Byron Katie's book, please summarize her wisdom in your own words, to help you to apply her wisdom to your life.

And as you read Byron Katie's book, please realize that the importance of Byron Katie's wisdom is its ability to increase our understanding of the decisions we make in our lives that may be generating negative unfair feelings in our lives that we can learn to correct, by killing the errors in our thinking, to enable us to change any incorrect decisions about our lives to the truth and to enable us to stop generating future negative feelings, such as when we generate future fear, anger, worry & stress in our lives, when we falsely believe that people or events in our lives are generating the unfairness that are creating these painful feelings.

With the help of Byron Katie's wisdom, I am beginning to realize that I can increase the truth in my thinking by eliminating the errors that I find in my thinking, to become able to increase my positive life-enhancing feelings that are based on true decisions about my life, such as when I am able to increase the love & happiness that I share with my friends & family when I correct the errors in my thinking.

DISCLAIMER - This is my summary of the wisdom contained in Byron Katie's book, "Loving What Is" and does not necessarily reflect the views of Byron Katie. The quotes of Byron Katie's wisdom have been modified to the first person singular tense and my words have been added to modify her words to help me to relate her wisdom to my life.

I am using a modified version of Byron Katie's Wisdom to find the truth or the errors contained in my feelings, thoughts & images that are living in my conscious mind about the Original Decisions that I make about the events in my life, especially the original decisions I make about my friends & family

An Original Decision is defined as the forming of an evaluation, opinion, estimate, notion or conclusion about the truth of the events in my life that I add to The Story of My Life that I create in my mind each day. These events live inside my conscious mind as my feelings, thoughts & images of the external world, my dreams, my memories & my thinking.[78]

To help me understand My Original Decisions. I am answering a modified version of Byron Katie's Questions to help me find the truth that may be hidden inside my decisions about the events in my life. These modified questions I call,

**The Questions for Truth**

I am answering the questions for truth to understand, "What is creating this?" about every mental activity in my conscious mind to become able to judge what is real. [83]

1) Are the feelings, thoughts & images in my mind a true description of my past, present or future life?

2) How do I test my feelings, thoughts & images for truth?

3) What impact will a revised decision about the truth or untruth of a feeling, thought or image have on my life?

4) How do I ask for forgiveness when I hurt someone or I hurt my life by making an **untrue** Original Decision?

Please ask The Questions for Truth about any decision that you may have regretted making in the past and then reread the Visualizing Myself as a Teenager section in The Introduction section of Our Book Two. In this section I asked you to practice forgiving someone who hurt you unfairly. Now, I recommend that you use the same five steps to emotional freedom to practice forgiving yourself for an incorrect decision that you regret making in your life.

I have included a list of incorrect decisions that many of us have made in our lives and that some of us may still be making, when we have difficulty admitting that we made a wrong decision and then have difficulty forgiving ourselves for making a wrong decision.

1) Forgiving myself for pretending to be someone I am not to impress someone falsely so they will like me more, such as a potential lover or a boss at work and then being caught lying about myself.

2) Forgiving myself for hurting a friend.

3) Forgiving myself for not making a career change or for refusing a job that I would have enjoyed doing.

4) Forgiving myself for procrastinating about an important decision in my life.

5) Forgiving myself for spending or wasting money that I could have saved and then spent on something more worthwhile.

6) Forgiving myself for believing that life is being unfair to me when I lose a loved one.

(Please refer to Step 4 of the Nine Steps to Emotional Freedom section in Chapter 13 of Our Book One)

7) Forgiving myself for missing opportunities for new fun & adventures.

8) Forgiving myself for not loving a friend or family member enough to forgive them.

9) Forgiving myself for not completing my education.

10) Forgiving myself for the mistakes I made as a parent.

11) Forgiving myself for misjudging someone.

12) Forgiving myself for not achieving a goal in my life.

13) Forgiving myself for treating someone unfairly after I ask them for forgiveness and try to make amends for the pain & suffering that I have caused.

To be able to forgive myself, I am using the questions for truth, as needed, to help evaluate all the decisions I make about the feelings, thoughts & images that enter my mind each day, so I can test them for truth and correct any errors in my thinking.


(Please refer to the Practicing Friendship to Understand Why a Feeling is Being Created section in Step 2 of The Nine Steps in Chapter 13 of Our Book One)

This Turnaround Process to achieve forgiveness starts when I take my original decision that I believe is true and then I turn it around, to the opposite decision, to another alternative decision, or to accepting personal responsibility for the causes of a decision, to stop me from blaming others for the errors contained in my thinking about the events in my life that I have stored in my memories.

Then, I use the revealed truth that the turnaround process provides me to correct errors about the events in my life that are contained in my feelings, thoughts & images that I am storing in my memories, to prevent me from using these errors in my future life to hurt my friends or family when I make a mistake because I believe an error in my thinking is true, such as when I think a friend hates me until I use the turnaround process and I begin to realize that she actually loves me and wants to be my friend once again. My error was not realizing that she was just angry with me and she has now forgiven me, even though I do not deserve her love & forgiveness because of my bad behavior that caused her to become upset with me.

**Practicing Turning Around the Errors in My Thinking**

The purpose of the turnaround process is to question the beliefs stored in my memories of the events in my life by using the questions for truth to find out if my original decisions about these events in my life are true or false, by turning around my decision about the events and by looking at the circumstances supporting my decision in different ways to test my original decision for truth. And if it contains errors, to kill the errors in my thinking & my memories to enable me to make a revised & correct decision that is based on the truth of the circumstances, after I have killed the errors in my thinking & my memories by;

Turning Around my original decision of what I believe to be true to the opposite decision that it may be false when I ask "What if it is false?" as I try to understand the impact that my changed belief has on my life.

Or, turning around my original decision of what I believe to be false to the opposite decision that it may be true when I ask "What if it is true?" as I try to understand the impact that my changed belief has on my life.

For Example:

If I changed the belief that there is no God in the universe to the belief that there is a God and then I can use the turnaround process to ask, "What impact does my new belief in a universal creator have on my life?"

I may also use the turnaround process to challenge my beliefs, such as, when I believe there is no life after death, a belief that is generating my fear of growing old & dying.

This is the process of turning around my original decision of what I believe is true or false to another alternative decision by asking, "What alternatives to my belief are possible?" and then by asking, "What impact does a revised decision or a new alternative way of looking at the circumstances supporting my original decision, have on my life, if it is different from my original decision about life?"

For Example:

If I blamed my neighbor's children for throwing a rock that cracked my car windshield, while it was sitting overnight in the driveway in front of my house, I would look for other alternatives because I did not see the person who threw the rock. I may ask myself, "Do the neighbor's children deserve my fair decision that they are innocent until proven guilty?" or I may ask, "Who else may have broken the car window?" and "How can I find the truth about what happened?"

Turning around my original decision of what I believe is true or false by taking responsibility for the circumstances causing the decision, onto my self, will help to correct any errors in my thinking when I may be trying to blame another person for unfair or painful events in my life.

If I blamed My Son for not spending more time with me, I will hopefully realize that his university workload is heavy and he has little spare time to spend with his Dad. And then I may ask, "Have I been creating unfair pain in our lives because of my unrealistic expectation that my son has enough extra spare time to spend with his Dad?"

After I do the turnaround process once again and I revise my original decision of the situation, I am looking at my revised decision and I am asking if it is as true or truer than the original decision that I held in my mind when I first asked, "Is it true or false?"

## Understanding The Turnaround Process

The power of the turnaround lies in the discovery that everything I think I see in the outside world becomes the story of my life that I create inside my own mind. As I try to create a mirror image of the outside world inside my mind, I may make an incorrect interpretation of the events in my life that are occurring in the outside world. [79]

I observe everything that lives outside of me by building an image of this outside world inside my conscious mind. The image I build inside my mind becomes The Story of My Life, to which I add new chapters containing the new events in my life that I experience during each new day of future life. I become the storyteller of my life, the creator of all my stories, and the world I create inside my mind is my created image of what I observe in the real outside world. Unfortunately, my understanding of what I have observed may be wrong [80]

Practicing The Turnaround Process points me to the truth of who I am, without any false stories of what I have experienced in my life. It's all done for me by the turnaround process. [81]

Then, I may practice forgiveness to enable me to use the power of forgiveness to kill any quilt that I may feel, whenever I practice the turnaround process and I began to realize that my negative decisions about my life are the causes of many of my negative feelings, such as when I stop believing in my memory of an incorrect story of my life that has been generating negative pain & suffering in my life, when I keep reliving a negative memory about my friends & family that is not true.

(Please refer to the Practicing Forgiveness to Prevent an Unfair Memory from Creating Pain section in Step 5 of The Nine Steps in Chapter 13 of Our Book One)

By adopting the wisdom of answering the questions for truth and doing the turnaround process, I have retaken the ownership of the feelings, thoughts & images that enter my conscious mind each day by realizing that I can manage all my feelings because I am solely responsible for generating the thinking energy that my feelings are using to keep themselves alive in my mind. Then I can decide to use the thinking energy that I control to generate either pain & suffering or joy & happiness in my future life. The choice is solely mine to make.

And when I do **not** practice the turnaround process to look for the truth in my life, I start to live In A Dream World of My Life that may not be true.

I may start living inside A Bubble of Protection where I only want to feel joy & happiness and I want my life to always be fair to me. Then, I may try to **not** allow pain & suffering into My Bubble of Protection by continuously suppressing my memories of the pain & suffering that I have experienced in my past life whenever I cannot stop my memories from hurting me.

Unfortunately, unfair pain & suffering continues to enter My Bubble of Protection whenever I relive a painful memory that I cannot stop reliving. Then these painful memories that I cannot stop reliving, start to clash with my dream world, as my dream world starts to clash with what is, which is the real world that contains my painful unfair memories that I do not want to feel, as I begin to realize that "my thoughts are arguing with reality" [82] as the pain & suffering in my life continues and I do not know how to stop my memories of pain & suffering from hurting me.

Fortunately, I have the opportunity to learn to manage my feelings of pain & suffering by realizing that when I do not accept reality, as it is, then I start to hurt, whenever I suppress my memories of pain & suffering in my life instead of learning how to accept reality, as it is, by accepting that I can learn to manage my pain & suffering and then I can learn how to kill the pain & suffering so it cannot hurt me again in the future by practicing forgiveness, so my memories will no longer generate pain & suffering into my future life.

I am learning to accept what is and to get on with what I can manage, to enable me to generate increasing love, peace, joy & compassion in my life by forgiving those who have caused the unfair pain & suffering in my past life and by forgiving me when I realize that I am the cause of the unfair pain & suffering in my present life.

Unfortunately, I recreate my dream world & the false story of my life whenever I start to believe a feeling, thought or image that is wrong, without checking or inquiring, to find out if the thought is true or not. Then, I start to feel new pain & suffering in my future life, such as when I start to believe untrue thoughts about my family, my friends & my relationships, as these thoughts become new errors in my thinking. To stop any potential unfair pain & suffering from occurring in the future, I am learning how to spot each new error in my thinking and then I am learning how to kill the errors in my thinking so they cannot start to generate new unfair pain & suffering in my future life.

**Finding the Truth in My Thinking**

"I am writing down the feelings, thoughts & images about the stories of my life that are running through my conscious mind, the ones that really cause me pain including my anger, resentment & sadness. I am pointing my finger of blame, first at the people who have hurt me.

Every story of my life is a variation on a single theme that this shouldn't be happening and that I shouldn't have to experience this, that God is unjust & that my life is unfair. When I believe that my family or my friends are causing me pain, I am filling out "The Judge My Neighbor Worksheet" that is offered free on Byron Katie's website, to help me to understand my painful story & my decisions about the persons who I believe are causing me pain. The worksheet is designed to draw out my decisions that otherwise might be difficult to uncover.

Then, once again, I ask the questions for truth about each new story that enters my future life as I begin to use the turnaround process to find out the truth about the decisions that I have made in my new story of my life, as I write about the experiences in my life in a personal private file on my computer.

Then, I am closing my eyes and imagining me for a moment not believing that the decisions are true. I am imagining me standing in front of the people or in the same situations when I made the original decisions, when I think about the decisions I have made. How did I react? How did I feel? What did I see? Then, I am writing down what I & my life will become when I no longer believe the decisions are true.

As I write about my friends & family in the new story of my life, I am imagining that each person is me. I am now that person. How do I react when I am treated by someone who believes this decision is true? Is the decision true? Is my accuser correct? Is my accuser telling me something that I may not want to hear?

**Turning Around My Life Experiences to the Truth**

I have three choices to turn around the stories of my life to the truth when I realize:

1) A decision about my life experience can be turned around by imagining that the decision is not true.

2) A decision about my life experience can be turned around by finding an alternative cause for the decision.

3) A decision about a life experience can be turned around by me, by taking responsible for the life experience whenever I blame another person for the experience or when a random event in my life creates the experience that is no one's fault.

After I do the turnaround process once and then rewrite my revised decisions into a new story of my life, then I must be willing to go inside each revised decision and ask if it is true or truer than the original decision that I wrote down when I first asked, "Is it true?" The power of the turnaround process lies in the discovery that everything that I think I see in the outside world becomes a true or false story of my life that I create in my own mind.

Everything is a fabricated image of the external world that I create in my own mind and when I change this created image in my mind, I can change the decision & my image of external reality.

Everything outside of me is created in my mind by my feelings thoughts & images. I am the storyteller & the creator of all the stories of my life, and the stories I create inside my mind are based on my decisions about the outside world. The turnaround process is my reentry into the truth in my life, as the truth points me to Who I Am, when I no longer believe a story containing untrue decisions that cause me pain, when I falsely believe that they are true. It's all done for me.

(Please refer to The Mirror in My Mind section in Chapter 22 of Our Book One)

The Turnaround Process includes the part where I take what I have written about others, so I can decide if it is true or truer when it applies to me, as I pretend to be that person.

As long as I think that the cause of my problem is "out there" and as long as I think that anyone or anything else is responsible for my suffering, then the situation becomes hopeless. It means that I am forever in the role of the victim.

Byron Katie's wisdom brings the truth home to me, to enable me to understand how I am helping to cause the unfair pain in my life and how I can set myself free from my unfair pain & suffering. Inquiry combined with the turnaround process is the fast track to my realization of the truth of my involvement in producing the unfair pain and is the fast track to the knowledge of the truth, as I learn what will enable me to end the unresolved pain & suffering in my life.

My realization is not complete until my revealed truth lives as action, as I begin to live my turnarounds to the truth.

To enable me to live the truth in the story of my life, I am finding three genuine examples of how my life will change to truth, as I begin the turnaround process, when I no longer believe my decisions are true. The turnaround process is my prescription for health, peace & happiness, as I get rid of all untrue decisions about the persons or events that are causing the unfair pain in my life.

Then, I use Reporting as another powerful way that I have found to enable me to manifest my realization of my turn around, as I change my life to the truth, when I go to the persons who I have judged unfairly with my untrue & negative thoughts and I share my turnarounds & realizations. I report only what I have discovered about my part in keeping the negative untrue thoughts alive in my life that generate the unfair pain & suffering. Under no circumstances do I talk about their part in keeping my negative untrue thoughts alive.

My Reporting makes me realize that I am starting to live in a state of continuous love, peace, joy & compassion as I start to become the unconditionally loving human being who I was born to be and as I start to no longer believe any untrue stories of my life. Now, I am using the renewed unconditional love of my childhood to ask,

Can I just live my life without judging other people and blaming them for my unfair pain & suffering?

Then, I am going through my list of written decisions describing the persons who I have hurt unfairly.

How did I react and how did I treat them unfairly when I believed my untrue & negative thoughts?

I am relieving my unfair pain & suffering by making apologies, asking for forgiveness & offering compensation, to all those who I have hurt." (Modified quote of Byron Katie's wisdom)

**Helping My Friends & Family**

I am answering the questions for truth about every belief that I hold, especially when I start to believe in my thoughts that life is being unfair to me, when I think my friends & family are betraying my trust & my love for them.

(Please read the example of a friend who betrayed my trust in the How I Nurture True Friendship section in Chapter 22 of Our Book One to observe how I started using The Turnaround Process by asking myself, "Is it True")

When I started practicing Byron Katie's wisdom by asking quality questions about my thoughts to identify the errors in my thinking, I was able to identify the negative feelings that I held about each member of my family, friends, neighbors, & co-workers that were being generated in my life, each day, by my mistakes & my false beliefs about their characters, because I falsely believed that the errors in my thinking were true.

Now that I am correcting these errors, I am able to love my friends & family more passionately and I am beginning to realize that the beliefs I hold about the character of a member of my family or a friend, may be wrong. They may be more loving & supportive then I realize, when they hurt me unfairly, especially when I start to generate a mistaken belief in my thinking about their lack of love & support for me.

This is why it is so important for me to ask the questions for truth about my relationships.

I may feel unfair pain & suffering when my friends & family treat me unfairly, but I am beginning to realize that when I check these feelings for truth and I find they are based on errors in my thinking, my mind will accept my corrections and end my feelings of unfair pain & suffering. Then, my relationships with my friends & family will be based on truth and not based on my imagined dream world that I sometimes construct in my mind when a family member or a friend treats me unfairly.

Now, I realize that one of several possible events may have happened in a relationship to cause new unfairness in my life.

My friends & family may be angry with me for something I said or did to them and they will probably forgive me, as long as I have not hurt them too severely. Then, they will start loving me once again, as long as I ask for their forgiveness, as I convince myself to get out of my imagined dream world as I start checking my painful feelings and my thinking for errors, so I can understand why I have treated them unfairly, even though the unfairness may be a result of a misunderstanding between us.

My friends & family may be temporarily treating me unfairly because they are imagining things about my character that are untrue, so they have become angry with me, especially when they feel I owe them more love & respect.

And my friends & family may be temporarily allowing their Egos to control them when they want something from me and I am unwilling to give it to them, so they start treating me as their adversary and they start hurting me on purpose to satisfy their Egos need for justice or revenge, when they do not get what they want from me.

(Please refer to The Wisdom of Children is Hazardous to My Ego! section in Chapter 18 of Our Book One)

This is reality that I can only see & understand when I correct the mistaken beliefs in my thinking. When I begin to see & understand the truth, the truth enables me to start generating more love, peace, joy & compassion in my relationships, once again.

Now, I realize that any new unfair pain & suffering in my relationships with my friends & family can be eliminated, by realizing that I can kill the errors in my thinking and I can forgive my friends & family for any errors in their thinking that they make, when then they treat me unfairly.

Now, I no longer believe that my friends & family will continue to be unfair to me, such as refusing to help me when I need them, or not loving me enough, or not being supportive enough, or not understanding my needs, or not listening to me enough, because I realize that my feelings of unfair treatment by my friends & family may be generated by the errors in our thinking and once we correct these errors, we will start to love each other more passionately, once again.

Now, I realize the truth about my friends & family. The truth is they will love & support me because I can now feel the powerful unconditional love that is living in their hearts that they will use to love me, except when they are angry with me or they start to treat me unfairly.

I am beginning to realize that underneath their pain & angry is their Internal Source of Unconditional Love that may be temporarily blocked by their suffering, when they are being unfair to me.

And I realize that the mistaken beliefs in my thinking may not have allowed me to understand or see the love that they have for me in their hearts.

Now that I can feel the love in their hearts, once again, I am beginning to realize that when we were born as babies, we were born as unconditional loving human beings who were in love with all the life around us and who felt loved by all this life, as we felt immense love for our friends & family. This childhood ability to love our friends & family is still in our adult hearts. As adults we are capable of learning how to start offering this powerful love, once again, to our friends & family.

But first, before becoming able to do this, we need to realize that many of us have diminished or lost the power of our childhood ability to love life passionately because this ability is being blocked by the errors in our thinking or by the unresolved pain & suffering in our lives that we do not know how to stop hurting us.

Fortunately, when we were babies we did not have these errors in our thinking and we did not have unfair painful memories about our friends & family, as we unconditionally loved all human beings in our life with intense unreserved passion.

Unfortunately, by the time we became adults, many of us became unable to unconditionally love other human beings and our love became totally conditional, when we withdrew our love from our friends & family, when they treated us unfairly.

(Pease refer to the Forgiving the Unresolved Pain & Suffering in My Life section in Chapter 3 Our Book One for an explanation of how many of us slowly lose our ability to passionately love life as we grow from childhood into teenagers and then adults)

Now that I am practicing Byron Katie's wisdom, I am using her wisdom to help each member of my friends & family who may be feeling unfair pain & suffering and who does not know how to stop these negative feelings from hurting.

Such as, when I offer my support to a loved one as she recovers from the pain & suffering of a broken romantic relationship, by helping her to ask the questions for truth about her relationship, by helping her to clean out any mistaken beliefs from her mind about her love relationship.

And I can help her to fully reconnect to her childhood internal source of unconditional love, so she becomes able to forgive her ex-lover, even though her lover may not deserve forgiveness for unsetting her & treating her unfairly. She does not have to tell her lover that she has forgiven him. However, the forgiveness will help her to feel less unresolved pain & suffering in the future whenever she thinks about him, though it may take months or years for her to fully forgive him, depending on how badly she has been hurt.

The turnaround process & the questions for truth help us to love our friends & family and help us to learn to correct the mistaken beliefs that we hold in our thoughts & memories about our relationships, as we try to increase the unconditional love that we share with our friends & family.

Please remember that all human beings are automatically fully reconnected to their childhood internal source of unconditional love when they remove the mistaken beliefs or the unresolved pain & suffering in their minds that may be blocking this connection. Feeling continuous unconditional love for all life is our natural state of being that we were born possessing and this state is always ours & can never be taken away from us. In Our Book One we asked you to prove the truth of this wisdom by remembering when you felt powerful unconditional love for all the life that surrounded you, especially the love for your friends & family, when you were a child.

Fortunately, the enhanced wisdom in Our Book Two helps us to increase our ability to feel this unconditional love, once again, when we are adults. Our unconditional love can be hidden from us by our mistaken beliefs and the questions for truth will help us to correct these mistakes, so we can fully reconnect to our childhood ability to unconditionally love our friends & family with great passion.

And we can also stop our unfair painful memories from hurting us in the future by practicing the wisdom in the Killing Unfairness to Achieve Emotional Freedom section in Chapter 11 of Our Book One.

**Byron Katie's Wisdom for Embracing Reality**

"When I practice answering the questions for truth, I begin to realize that "All the stress that I will feel in the future may be caused by arguing with what is. When I argue with reality I lose. I am a lover of what is because it hurts when I argue with reality.

I can only find three kinds of business in the universe, mine, yours and God's, who is reality. Everything that is out of my control, your control & everyone else's control is God's business. Being mentally in your business keeps me from being present in my own business. Life is so simple when I move back into my own business.

A thought is harmless until I believe it, when it is not true. It's not my thoughts but my mental attachment to the thought that causes my suffering, when the thought is not true.

Attaching to a thought means believing it is true without inquiring. A belief is a thought that I am attached to without inquiring whether the thought is true or not. Thoughts just appear. They come out of nothing and go back to nothing. There is no harm in thoughts until I attach to them when they are wrong, when I don't let go of thoughts. So, I am meeting them with the questions for truth to find & correct the errors they contain when they first appear inside my conscious mind. Then my potential future unfair pain & suffering that would be caused by these new untrue thoughts let's go of me, as these untrue thoughts disappear from my conscious mind because I do not attach to them.

Stories of my life are the untested, uninvestigated theories that tell me what all things mean to me in my life. I don't often realize that they're just theories. When I'm operating on uninvestigated theories of what's going on, and I'm not even aware of it, I'm in what I call My Dream World.

I have never experienced a stressful feeling that wasn't caused by attaching to an untrue thought. For example, the untrue thought that life is being unfair to me is buried inside all my memories of the unfair pain & suffering in my past life. Behind every uncomfortable feeling, there's a thought that isn't true for me, such as the untrue thought that my future life will be unfair to me.

When I have a thought that argues with reality, then I have a stressful feeling. Rather than understand my thoughts that are buried inside my original decision about the event, by looking inside my mind, I may try to change my stressful feeling by looking outside of me, so I can lose myself in the outside world, as I try to reduce my stress level by not thinking about the stress buried inside my memory of an unfair event in my life that is generating this stress and by trying to suppress my feeling of stress, as I try to ignore my stress. When I look into the outside world, I'm caught in my dream world that I use to escape from the worry, stress, fear & anger in my mind, as I start living a story of my life that isn't true for me because I am trying to believe that the unresolved pain & suffering in my mind does not exist.

Investigating an untrue thought will always lead me back to who I really am. It hurts to believe that I'm other than who I really am.

When I allow my stress to become part of the true story of my life and then I start looking for the causes of my stress, I become able to kill any untrue thoughts that I may find, to help me to live a true story of my life that enables me to create happiness in my life.

Once I understand through inquiry that an untrue thought is causing me suffering, I detach myself from it.

(Please refer to the Practicing Detachment section in Step One of The Nine Steps in Chapter 13 of Our Book One)

Before the thought I wasn't suffering, with the thought I'm suffering, and when I realize that the thought isn't true, my suffering stops.

This is how asking & answering the questions for truth to correct the errors in my thinking works. This is my understanding of why Byron Katie calls this process The Work.

Inquiry invites me into an awareness of cause & effect. Once I recognize this, all my suffering begins to unravel on its own, when I realize a thought is untrue.

I use Inquiry in the same way that I use The Turnaround Process & The Work. To inquire or to investigate is to put a thought or a story of my life up against the questions for truth and then I turnaround my story to the truth, by correcting the errors in my story, which becomes The Work in progress.

Inquiry is a way to end the confusion that is blocking my ability to experience powerful love, peace, joy & compassion for all the life around me, especially for my friends & family.

Inquiry is about realizing that all the answers that I will ever need are always available inside of me. Love, peace, joy & compassion naturally, inevitably & irreversibly make their way into every corner of my mind & body and into every relationship & experience.

I am either attaching to my thoughts without asking, Are they true? or I am inquiring about the truth of my thoughts. There's no other choice and I am finding that even the most unpleasant thoughts can be met with unconditional love.

My mind recreates what I observe in outside world and this mental recreation becomes a true picture or a true video of the events that I experience in the outside world that lives inside of my mind, as A True Re-Creation of the Outside World inside My Mind, as long as I record true feelings, thoughts or images about the events that occur in the real world outside of me when I am creating this story of my life. I am the storyteller and the creator of all the stories of my life, so I have to be careful not to create A Dream World Inside My Mind that contains untrue feelings, thoughts & images about the events I experience in my life.

When I realize that every stressful moment that I experience is a gift that points me to the errors in my thoughts and when I realize how to correct my errors so I can gain my own freedom from unfair pain & suffering, then my life becomes very kind." (Modified quote of Byron Katie's wisdom)

### Adding Free Will to Byron Katie's Wisdom

In the next section of our summary of Byron's Katie's wisdom we have included the concept of Free Will to make it easier for us to begin to apply Byron Katie's wisdom to our lives, so that her wisdom will start to bond with our existing personal wisdom that we use in our daily lives, a personal wisdom that we have proven to be true in our life experiences.

DISCLAIMER – Our concept of Free Will does not necessarily reflect the views of Byron Katie.

"In the future, when I realize that my unfair pain & suffering is calling me to Inquiry, then I am beginning to look forward to my uncomfortable feelings. I am beginning to experience them as friends, as they tell me about my untrue thoughts that I can correct, to stop my unfair pain & suffering. The process of answering the questions for truth is helping me to kill all my untrue thoughts that are generating unfair pain & suffering in my life, that are preventing me from reconnecting to my internal source of unconditional love which contains abundant love, peace, joy & compassion.

When I see that it is only my thinking that I am learning to question, then every problem that I experience becomes a joy when I use the questions for truth, to correct the errors in my thinking, to be able to replace my suffering & pain with peace, joy, happiness & compassion.

Life is a very nice place to be once I understand it. Nothing ever needs to go wrong in my life. My life becomes heaven on Earth, except when I attach to untrue stories that I have not investigated.

When I become a lover of what is, there are no more important decisions for me to make to understand my life, I just wait & watch. I know that the important decisions that bring increased joy & happiness into my life will be made in their own time. So, I let go of when, where & how. All my important choices are made for me.

The parts of me that I label with the concepts called, My Conscience, My Compassionate Watcher, My Soul & My Spiritual Being are different names for The Pure Eternal Spiritual Energy of the Universe that energizes me and that guides me all day long, to make true & correct choices that offer to bring increased joy & happiness into my life. I am really alive when I live simply by not attaching to any untrue stories, as I live in the continuous present moment of my life. I am trusting, loving & waiting to do whatever simple task that appears in front of me. As I wait to make decisions about my life, I lead a simple life that unfolds before me, always by divine guidance.

I never receive more choices to make than I can handle. There is always just one choice to make at a time, as I make my decisions to manage the truth in my life or to follow the mistakes in my thinking. I use my Free Will to choose the truth or untruth and the right or wrong, an ability that God has given me. I have faith that I have been put on Earth to practice My Free Will to either think true thoughts that bring increased joy & happiness into my life or to think untrue thoughts that bring increased pain & suffering into my life. My life never gets more difficult than that because I do not let an untrue story of how this or that will impact my future life or intrude into my present life when I am doing each simple task that my daily life requires. I just make each simple choice to improve my well-being by choosing the correct thought with My Free Will to guide my actions and by enjoying each simple task that God offers me each day of my life.

Then, the only future that I want to experience becomes filled with love, peace, joy & compassion. Who cares if I am rich or poor when I am secure in my spiritual happiness? This is true freedom when I am no longer deceived by my untrue thoughts. New thoughts appear, stay for a while in my mind & then disappear during each day of my life.

How am I going to meet them when they first appear in my conscious mind? That is all that is happening here. I am either attaching to an uninvestigated thought or I am answering the questions for truth to attach to a true thought. That is my daily experience. I choose the true or untrue thoughts that I am being offered. God makes the choices available for me to choose with My Free Will. I do not bother trying to make true thoughts because I have Faith that they will be made for me, right on time, when I need them. My job is to be at peace in the present moment and wait until I am asked to make a decision with My Free Will to manage my thinking, by choosing true thoughts, or by following my untrue thoughts when I do not investigate them with the questions for truth.

My decisions are easy. It is the untrue story that I tell with my untrue thoughts that generates future pain in my life. So, I just enjoy the experience of living each day of my life until I have to make the next decision, which is a choice between truth and error! And that is my position. I am a lover of what is. My life offers me choices of when to eat, when to sleep & when to act. It just moves along on its own and it is very calm & very successful, as it offers me all that I need to be able to choose the correct & true thoughts that bring increasing joy & happiness into my life each day.

Making the correct decisions requires an understanding of the way my mind works and requires me to ask the questions for truth, so I can apply the resulting true answers to my life. This process of finding the truth in my life is not about changing anything in the world. The world is as I perceive it to be. For me "The Clarity of Truth" is a phrase for experiencing beauty in my life. The pure eternal spiritual energy of the universe is what I am, and when I am clear about the truth in my life, I am able to experience love & beauty in my life. Nothing else is possible. I am a field of pure eternal spiritual energy who accepts my true thoughts and everything unfolds from that. When my thoughts are not clear & not truthful, I start to project the insanity of my untrue thoughts out into the world as this insanity becomes my understanding of the world. Then, I falsely create an insane world inside my mind and I may falsely start to think that the world is the source of my unfair pain & suffering.

Human beings have been analyzing their perceptions of the world for thousands of years and have not been doing enough analyzing of the errors contained in their thinking, when they label their perceptions of the world falsely. When I meet my thoughts with clarity & truth, the world becomes sane because I am now sending the sanity of true thoughts out into the world and receiving the sanity of truth back from the world. My challenge and one of the goals of my life is to help my friends & family to allow only true thoughts into their image of the world that they are creating in their minds.

I am doing what my love for all the life that surrounds me requires me to do, by answering the questions for truth about the truth in all my feelings, thoughts & images, to keep me sane and to keep me enjoying a loving & happy life. That is the purpose of my stress. It has become my friend. It has become an alarm clock that is built into me that tells me when it is time to ask questions about the truth of my thoughts that are causing me stress. So, I am investigating my thoughts to correct my mistaken thinking and then, I am returning to being who I am meant to be, as an unconditional loving person who only allows true thoughts into my life that generate joy & love.

And when I accept falsehoods as truth, I am no longer who I am not meant to be, as I become a neurotic person who allows untrue thoughts into my life that create unresolved pain & suffering. This is what is happens to me when I use My Free Will to become a sane or neurotic human being. It is my choice.

It is only my story of untrue thoughts that keeps me from knowing that I always have everything that I need, to bring increasing happiness into my life. My untrue story becomes my gift, when I analyze it by answering the questions for truth to become able to kill all the untrue thoughts in the story of my life and to stop all my personal self-inflicted unfair pain & suffering, so I can become able to fully reconnect to my internal source of unconditional love and become able to rest in the Arms of God & Just Be, as I make choices with My Free Will each new day of my life.

I am looking for unconditional love in all the choices I make, until I realize that unconditional love is what I am, inside of me, whenever I have been guilty of seeking true love, outside of me. True love is all that I have been looking for. It is what I already have inside of me whenever I fully reconnect to it and become a child, once again, as I share my unconditional love with everyone in my life as I did when I was a child.

The turnaround to unconditional love is my re-entry into a joyful & happy life as the truth points me to who I am as a human being, who no longer believes untrue stories about my life. It is all done for me. I am answering the questions for truth to allow this truth to live inside me.

As I kill the untruth in my mind, I begin to live my turnarounds to the truth by reporting my part to others, so I can hear the truth of my turnarounds as I make amends to those I have hurt, for the sake of my own freedom, to become able to increase the joy & happiness in my life.

Answering the questions for truth is speeding up the process of bringing freedom from pain & suffering into my life. Now, I realize that a lot of my unfair pain & suffering is caused by my attachment to deeply embedded mistaken beliefs. It is a state of blind attachment to thoughts that I falsely think are true.

When I learned to treat my thinking as a friend, I realized that I could treat every human being as a friend. What could I say that has not already appeared within me as a thought? The end of the war between me & my thinking is the end of the war within me. Then and only then can I fully reconnect to my internal source of unconditional love that gives me the power of forgiveness and takes away my need to seek justice from my friends & family, whenever they hurt me unfairly.

It is so simple. My mind can only find its true nature by correct thinking. Nothing else is possible. When I love my friends & family without conditions, I can see that there is nothing to forgive my friends & family for. I am no longer arguing with reality which means arguing with the story of my past hurts and arguing with my need for forgiveness. My war with my unresolved pain & suffering is over when I fully reconnect to my internal source of unconditional love, as my renewed compassion & forgiveness stops my desire to seek justice from my friends & family and stops my desire to create more  pain & suffering in my relationships until my desire for revenge is satisfied.

Seeing clearly through the eyes of unconditional love is the compassionate & forgiving resource that I use, to act in the kindest, most appropriate & most effective way. I create an image of the outside world in my mind when I create the story of my life. I am the story of who I think I am. I am for now, an uninvestigated story which has become my own myth that I am investigating to become able to find the truth in the story of my life.

My happiness is generated by my understanding of the truth in the story of my life and is it not beautiful? It is what is true for me until it is not. When it changes, I am answering the questions for truth about the change. When I ask & answer the questions, the truth is realized within me and any untruth gets undone. The truth meets the untruth and they join together in harmony, in the balance of the two halves that join together into the realization of what is true and what is not true.

I am now, free of major unfair pain & suffering. Now, love motivates all of my actions and in my experience, reality is always kind, as evidenced by The Law of Karma maintaining the balance of fairness in my life and in the lives of all human beings on Earth and I am beginning to experience continuous unconditional love at all times. My life is not only interesting, it is ecstatic! What I want is what I already have, when my true thoughts & actions are not separate, when they move as one, without conflict.

When my joy & happiness starts to decline, I write down my conflicted thoughts and ask the questions for truth to find the untrue thought that is stopping me from feeling the continuous unconditional love, peace, joy & compassion that I want to use to power my future joy & happiness, during each moment of every new day of my future life. I accomplish this by killing all the untrue thoughts in my thinking and all the untrue thoughts that are buried inside my unfair memories, to become able to restore my joy & happiness.

I find that life never falls short and does not require a future. Everything I need is always supplied in the present moment and I do not have to do anything for it. Why would I want something more or less, than what I have, even if it is painful? What I see, where I am, what I smell & taste & feel. It is all so fine. When I love my life this way, I do not want to change it. There is nothing more exciting than loving what is. God, as I use the word is another name for what is. I always know God's intention. It is exactly what is in every present moment. I do not have to question it anymore. I am no longer meddling in God's business. It is simple. And from that basis, it is clear that everything is perfect. The last truth that I call the last decision is, "God is everything. God is love." Human beings who fully understand this do not need the questions for truth because they are allowing only truth into the real world they create inside their minds which has become a world of pure reality.

All my concepts of truth eventually fall away. Every concept of truth is a distortion of what is. When I investigate, I embrace the last truth as I join with God & rest in his arms & just be. This peaceful state of connection with God is beyond all conceptual truths. It is true intimacy with God's realization of the unconditional love from all life that I feel. Only in this moment am I resting inside the pure reality of the present moment without any distortion from my thinking. I am learning to live in this pure present moment, to become able to love whatever is in front of me, to love it as me as I was born to be.

Then, as I keep answering the questions for truth, I am seeing more clearly who I am without a past or future. The miracle of unconditional love comes to me in the presence of the un-interpreted present moment, in the presence of God who is pure unconditional love. When I am mentally somewhere else, I miss real life.

But even the Now is a concept. Even as the thought of Now completes itself, it is gone with no proof that it ever existed, other than as a concept, whose memory leads me to believe that it existed. Reality always becomes the story of the past. Before I can grasp it, it is gone.

Human experience is constantly changing, even though the place of reality & truth never moves. I say, let me begin from where I am. How can I tell the truth, as it appears now, without comparing it to what was true, a moment ago? Ask me again later and I may have a different truthful answer. Yes, I can always tell what the truth is, right Now.

Being honest in the present moment is always a comforting thing. The only person I can hurt is me, when I start to believe an untrue story of my life, a story that I tell others about myself. What I falsely believe is the only way that I can hurt me or my friends & family. And I will continue to suffer when I do not ask the questions for truth and do not correct the errors in my thinking that are causing my unresolved painful feelings that I may be inflicting on others. All I know is that when I hurt and I ask & answer the questions for truth, the pain stops. Then, I become enlightened to this present moment and my mind merges with my heart and comes to see that it is united with the unconditional love that I am receiving from all the life in the universe, as I reconnect to God, as I experience God's presence inside me, as I start to feel God's love for me, and as I start to feel united with God.

My truth finds a home and it rests in me, as me. Until my story is met with the understanding of the truth in my life, there is no peace. I am a lover of what is, which is what I always have when I think true thoughts. I discover my preferences by noticing what it is that I am doing. Whatever I am doing that is my preference. I am investigating all my beliefs that are causing my suffering. When my internal world is free of unfair pain & suffering, it becomes wonderful as it fills me with love, peace, joy & compassion. Why would I want to change it? When my dream is a happy one, why would I want to wake up? And when my dreams are not happy, I am answering the questions for truth to find the errors in my thinking to stop my unfair pain & suffering, so I can start to share my renewed happiness with those I love, with my friends, family, neighbors and everyone else that I will meet & greet today." (Modified quote of Byron Katie's wisdom)

## Thanking Byron Katie for Her Wisdom

Each day as I practice Byron Katie's wisdom I feel blessed by Byron Katie as her wisdom helps me to experience the true reality of the never ending present moment, as I empower the events in my life by killing the errors in my thinking, to enable me to embrace the truth of the present moment with powerful passion & unconditional love for all the life that surrounds me, especially the love for my friends & family.

And each day of my life, I am asking:

Are the questions for truth helping me to find the truth in the story of my life experiences that I am creating inside my mind, as I look outside my mind at all the new events in my life that I am experiencing each day?

How many times do I ask the questions for truth during a typical day?

What are the benefits for my future joy & happiness when I answer The Questions for Truth? Q-158

## Killing My Bubble of Protection

Before I started Practicing The Wisdom of Children, the feelings, thoughts & images that entered my mind each day were filtered through My Bubble of Protection which surrounded my conscious mind as it tried to protect me from future pain & suffering. This was part of the defence mechanism that I had developed during my childhood when I did not know how to stop the unfair experiences in my life from hurting me again in the future, whenever I started to relive a memory of one of these painful experiences.

As a child, I realized that when I accepted a challenge in the real external world of people & events, I became vulnerable to being hurt when my efforts to achieve success were met with obstacles that generated short term suffering in my life, such as when my offers of unconditional love & friendship were rejected.

So, I started using My Bubble of Protection to always feel pleasure & to avoid feeling pain.

For example, whenever I started to procrastinate to avoid accepting a new challenge in the real external world, I allowed my untrue thoughts about possible failures in my future life to start feeding thinking energy to my procrastination to keep it alive inside my mind, as I started to feel continuous fear of the future that was being generated by my memories of past failures that kept telling me that I may fail again in the future, as I have done in the past.

To help reduce the amount of fear that I was feeling, whenever I did not know how to stop the fear from hurting me, I asked My Bubble of Protection to protect me from my fear of future failure or loss by indulging in pleasurable activities such as watching TV or playing music that helped my bubble of protection to block my fear, by enabling me to hide inside feelings of pleasure.

Then when I became an adult, I started asking & answering The Questions for Truth to help me dismantle my bubble of protection, so I would no longer use this avoidance strategy to prevent me from accepting new challenges in the real external world whenever I became afraid of potential future failure or afraid of the potential loss of my future joy & happiness.

To start dismantling my bubble of protection I used my answers to the questions for truth to help me kill the fear of future failure or loss that was living inside my conscious mind. And when the fear was gone from my conscious mind, my internal source of unconditional love automatically started to motivate me to venture outside of my bubble of protection into the real external world of people & events, to become able to share my unconditional love with everyone & everything in life, as I continued to use Byron Katie's wisdom to kill any new unfair pain & suffering, such as fear of loss or failure, whenever untrue or false fear based feelings, thoughts or images entered my future life, once again.

"Now, that I have learned to kill any new unfair pain & suffering that may enter my future life, I am looking forward to accepting new challenges in the real external world that were not possible for me to enjoy in the past, when I spent most of my free time hiding away in a make believe world inside My Bubble of Protection when I tried to hide from the external world of new challenges & responsibilities, as I tried to feed my mind pleasure & avoid pain, such as when I read an enjoyable novel because I was afraid of being hurt if I accepted a new adventure in the external world that would require me to leave my bubble of protection that I had erected around myself to protect me from possible future failure or rejection in the real external world of people & events, outside of my home.

Now, for the first time in many years, I have the motivation and the eagerness to accept exciting new challenges in the real external world outside my bubble of protection.

And I realize that all I have to do, to bring additional fun & joy into my life, as I accept new challenges in the external world, is to Practice Choosing My Feelings, as described in Step 6 of the Nine Steps to Emotion Freedom section in Chapter 13 of Our Book One, so I can stay connected to The Present Moment and not get lost in thinking about my past life or my possible future life, as I venture out into the real external world with the understanding that I am an unconditionally loving human being who was born to be successful when I face new challenges in the real external world, as I feel the unconditional love surrounding me from all the life that lives in the external world, a powerful love that will protect me from fear as I look forward to sharing new fun & adventures with my friends & family."

(Quote from The Three Steps to Freedom from Unfairness section in Chapter 25 of Our Book One)

Killing My Bubble of Protection also enables me to nurture true friendship as I begin sharing fun & joy in the real external world with those who love sharing new adventures with me.

**Nurturing True Friendship**

"The ability to nurture True Friendship exits between two human beings, who share unconditional love with each other, who enjoy sharing fun & adventures together, who support each other through painful life experiences, and who forgive each other for the unfair pain & suffering that they create in their friendship.

Your true friend may be a mom or dad, husband or wife, son or daughter, boyfriend or girlfriend, co-worker or playmate, child or senior citizen. The only prerequisite is their ability to love you unconditionally and to forgive you, when you mess up and betray the friendship. In return, you require the ability to accept the unconditional love, cherish it, and try not to betray it, by thoughtless acts or words that hurt your true friend.

True friendship occurs, when one human being offers unconditional love to another human being, who accepts the unconditional love and then offers unconditional love in return.[37]

Saint Aelred described true friendship eloquently he said, "A truly loyal friend sees nothing in his friend but his heart." [38]

Which I modify by saying to myself when I am with a true friend, "I see nothing in my true friend but his heart"

True friendship may occur in a few seconds in total silence, as two human beings look into each other's eyes for the first time, to see the unconditional love in each other's heart. A special bonding of true friendship starts to occur without words, as they are joined together by the primordial energy strings of the universe that are generating the energy of unconditional love for all life, that resides in the hearts of all human beings, such as the unconditional love that is merging the new friends together, spiritually. True friendship can only be offered by a human being who is connected to his internal source of unconditional love".

(Quote from The Nature of True Friendship section in Chapter 22 of Our Book One)

**How I Become a True Friend**

I am beginning to fill my life with increased unconditional love & true friendship, as I learn to apply the wisdom in Our Books One & Two to my life.

How do I become a true friend to my friends & family, so they will ask me to help them to understand The Wisdom of Children, so we can share emotionally rewarding fun & adventures, together?

To accomplish this, I am developing the ability to become a true friend as I perfect my mastery of answering the questions for truth about the quality of my relationships and the truth about the beliefs, that I hold about me, to determine the truth of who I am & who I am not, to increase my ability to offer true friendship to other human beings.

In Chapter 18 of Our Book Two, I will ask you to write, in your own words, your understanding of how your mind should work to help you to identify, who you are & who you are not. The process of question asking to determine how your mind should work is based on asking yourself the questions for truth, to find the truth in your feelings, thoughts & images that will help you to kill the worry, stress, fear & anger in your daily life, so that you can start to rest in peace and start to enjoy your life more & more each day, as you find the truth in your life and as you kill the untruth in your life, to enable you to accomplish the true goals of your life and to enable you to increase your ability to share unconditional love & nurture true friendship with those you love.

**Re-Programming My Mind with Truth**

How do I ask my mind to help me ask & answer the questions for truth so I can start to reprogram all the errors in my thinking & all the errors in my unfair painful memories, to help me kill all the worry, stress, fear & angry that my thinking & my memories may be creating in my daily life?

And how do I ask my mind to help me fully reconnect to My Internal Source of Unconditional Love that I was born with, so I can start to continuously rest in love, peace, joy & compassion, each moment of every day of my future life, as I work on my goals to fulfill the purpose of my life?

The events I have experienced in life and my daily feelings, thoughts & images, have been stored as memory seeds in my mind, like data is stored on a computer hard drive.

**Managing My Sprouted Memory Seeds**

To manage my sprouted memory seeds, I am Practicing Friendship that is described in Step 2 of the Nine Steps to Emotional Freedom section in Chapter 13 of Our Book One, to help me understand why a feeling, thought or image is being created inside my conscious mind as I examine my attraction to the positive feelings of love peace, joy & compassion in my positive memories, or as I examine my aversion to the negative feelings of unresolved pain & suffering contained in my negative unfair memories, or as I examine my lack of desire due to my ignorance about a situation that generates neutral feelings from a sprouted neutral memory.

I have a choice at the moment of arising of a sprouted memory in my conscious mind as I use the questions for truth to help me decide if the memory is true & beneficial to me or untrue & harmful to me, before I make the decision to either enhance the power of a beneficial memory by indulging in thinking about it or I make the decision to cut off my thinking energy that is feeding a life-diminishing memory to kill its ability to distract me from working on my goals for the day.

How do I practice managing my sprouted memory seeds, to become able to increase the love, peace, joy & compassion in my life that I can share with my friends & family? Q-159

# Chapter 2

## Killing the Unfair Pain in My Memories

During my lifetime, when I agree with one of my memories that life has been unfair to me because someone hurt me by lying to me, by insulting me, by abusing me, by stealing from me, or by trying to manipulate me, I use my compassion to forgive the person who created the pain that is stored in my unfair memory, even though the person who hurt me may not deserve it.

Then, whenever this painful memory enters my mind in the future, I acknowledge this unfairness by telling my memory that I understand why my memory is causing me pain so it can get my attention, so it can tell me that this person may hurt me again the future. As this happens I greet my painful memory as a friend. Then, I tell my new friend that this person will not hurt me again in future. It only takes me a few seconds to make this statement to my memory as I ask my memory to stop causing me future pain to get my attention, to tell me that my future life may be unfair to me as it has been in the past because my life will be fair to me in the future and this person will not hurt me again in the future.

The agreement process that I use to convince my memories to stop causing me future pain, takes a lot longer for a painful memory that is much more intense and that may carry a tremendous amount of unfairness energy from my past life, such as the death of a loved one that I have known for years.

When my mother died during my teenage years, I became very angry with God for taking my mother away from me because it was so unfair to me & our family. Then, I kept adding new thinking energy to this unfairness whenever I remembered My Mom's death, as I carried this unfairness energy inside my heart for many years.

I was brought up as a Christian and attended Sunday school during my childhood and then I became an adult member of the local church, after taking the adult initiation course that was administered by the local clergy, when I was fourteen. I believed in God and I had a personal loving relationship with God.

That was why I was so upset and felt that God had betrayed me when my mother died because God did not help My Mom to become well again, to be able to continue loving me and to enable me to continue sharing unconditional love & true friendship with My Mom. The painful memory of the loss of My Mom intensified over the years, as I continually remembered and thought about how unfair her loss was to me and to our friends & family.

Eventually, I learned to forgive God and more importantly, to stop adding new unfair thinking energy to my painful memory of My Mom's death by stopping my compulsive thinking about the unfairness of my loss, when I learned from the wisdom of our ancestors that every time I thought that life was being unfair to me, I was giving the memory of the loss of My Mom new thinking energy that the memory was using to stay alive & active inside my conscious mind, new energy that it was using to continue hurting me.

When I stopped thinking that life was being unfair to me, the unresolved pain & suffering in conscious mind, such as the unfair loss of My Mom, started to run out of energy, as it used up all the energy it had stored inside my subconscious mind and then it had no choice but to disappear from my conscious mind, when it had no energy left in my subconscious mind to generate new unfair pain inside my conscious mind.

I had to accept that unfairness will sometimes occur in my life and I may not know why it occurred or who is responsible for this unfairness. God may have had a reason for taking My Mom back to Heaven so early in her life but I may never know why this occurred.

However, I have learned how to kill any new unresolved pain & suffering that may be created in my life by a new unfair future event, whenever someone or some new event treats me unfairly again. Then, I am able to start killing this unfair pain in a new memory by not feeding new unfair thinking energy to the memory to stop giving it the energy that it needs to stay alive & active inside my conscious mind.

My Mom was a wonderful loving human being, who I keep alive inside my heart. I still do not know why My Mom died so early in her life, especially when her family so desperately needed her and depended on her for the powerful love that she gave all of us, free of charge. Now, the power of the pain of this unfairness that resided inside the memories of my mother's death is gone. I was able to use the wisdom of our ancestors to kill this pain forever, by stopping my thinking that the loss of My Mom was so unfair, to stop this feeling of unfairness from living inside my heart alongside my ongoing love for My Mom, a love that I am cherishing each new day of my adult life whenever I remember My Mom.

Now, my memories of my mother are of the enjoyable & fun times, that we experienced together. And the memory of my mother's death & her funeral are no longer able to cause me pain, because I no longer think about the unfairness of her death, to stop generating new unfair thinking energy that can be used by my memory of her loss to create new pain in my life.

However, I will always miss My Mom as I cherish the memories of My Mom, as my love for my Mom remains powerful inside me, as it should be. The enjoyable memories of my Mom are keeping her alive inside my heart as they continue to help motivate me to live a compassionate life as I try to help others, as My Mom did when she was with us on Our Precious Mother Earth.

**Answering The Questions for Truth**

When I want to kill the unfair pain in my memories, I answer the questions for truth about the events in my life that created these memories whenever I start to feel the pain from my past life that is being generated into my adult life by these memories. It may take me days, weeks or months to be able to start to reduce the pain buried in these memories, as I continue to answer the questions for truth to help me understand the truth or untruth that is contained inside a memory of a past event in my life, whenever I start to relive this memory in the future, as the answers to the questions for truth help me to reduce the amount of the unfair pain that I may start to experience, whenever I start to relive a memory of loss, failure or disappointment in my life.

Killing the Unfair Pain in My Memories is easy to understand but difficult to master. Please be patience with yourself as you learn to understand your painful memories, as you learn to make them your friends, as you kill their ability to cause you future pain, and as you begin to experience less unfair pain and more unconditional love in your life, each day.

(Please refer to The Nine Steps to Emotional Freedom section in Chapter 13 of Our Book One to help you to kill the unresolved pain & suffering in your life)

# Chapter 3

## Learning to Manage My Worrying Process

Worry is defined as tormenting myself with, or suffering from, disturbing unfair thoughts about the pain or loss that may occur in my future life.

The way to stop worrying is to look underneath the compulsive worrying process, to find the untrue thoughts that are causing the pain & suffering which is being created by my fear of future failure or loss. Many human beings worry about situations that they feel they have no control over, so they do not feel that they can control their worrying.

"It is reported that over 90% of what we worry about never happens. That means our negative worries have about a 10% chance of being correct." - Dr. Susan Jeffers

The source of many of my worries is my fear that someone or something will come into my future life and take away my joy & happiness.

When I am worrying about something that I feel I have no control over, I am trying to **not** accept that I have no control over my fear of future failure or loss that is being energized by my worrying and my compulsively thinking about my fear. When the worrying is triggered by someone or something that creates fear in my life, then I am answering the questions for truth to help me understand why I am worrying so much.

To me accomplish this, I am asking my worrying process to become my new friend so it will tell me what past event or what possible future event is creating the daily worrying inside my conscious mind, so I can learn how to stop thinking about how unfair a past event in my life was, or how a future event may create new unfairness in my life.

Even if I have no direct control over the external circumstances that I am worrying about, I do have the ability to manage my feelings, which gives me the ability to kill the unfair fear that is being created inside my conscious mind, whenever the worrying process makes me afraid of what may happen to me or to my friends & family in the future.

Once I understand the truth or untrue thoughts that are creating this worrying process, I am **not** feeding new thinking energy to my worrying about the potential unfairness in my future life, so this worrying process will not be able to obtain any new unfair thinking energy to feed itself, so it can start generating new fear into my conscious mind each day.

Then, I am watching my worrying run out of the available energy that it has stored in its energy reserve in my subconscious mind, until the worrying process has no energy left to create new fear inside my conscious mind in the future.

When my worrying runs out of energy, it disappears from my conscious mind forever, unless I start feeding new unfair thinking energy to my worrying process once again in the future, whenever I become afraid of a new unfair event that may occur in my future life.

To kill this new fear of possible future unfairness, I am practicing The Nine Steps to Emotional Freedom in Chapter 13 of Our Book One.

## Surrendering to God

"I can also ask God to help me to stop my compulsive thinking about the fear in my life.

When I surrender my fear to God, his love starts to generate joy & fairness in my life and this helps to give me the energy that I need to stop compulsively thinking about the fear in my life because I have decided to ask the divine intelligence of the universe that is guiding my life, to help me find future joy & fairness and bring increasing unconditional love into my life.

When I surrender to God I am surrendering to the feelings of unconditional love that I am receiving **from** all the life in the universe, which will help me to fully reconnect to my internal source of unconditional love **for** all the life on Our Precious Mother Earth. Then, I will become able to Rest in the Arms of God & Just Be as I rest in love, peace, joy & compassion during each new moment of my daily life without any need to compulsively think about anything that may generate new fear in my life.

**Making it God's Business**

I do not have to compulsively worry any longer because it is no longer my business to stop worrying about the possible unfairness in my future life. It is now God's business to ensure my future life will be fair to me so I no longer need to worry about anything. It is now God's job because I have asked him to do this for me." (Modified wisdom from Byron Katie)

**When I am an Atheist**

Unfortunately, when I am an Atheist I will not be able to use God's help. However, I can still fully reconnect to my internal source of unconditional love that I was born possessing to help provide me with the power & energy that I need to start killing my compulsive thinking about potential unfairness that may create new fear in my future life.

It is much easier to kill my compulsive thinking with God's help, so I may decide to re-read the discussion on The Choice to Acquire Faith section in Chapter 22 of Our Book One.

In the meantime, I am continuing to practice The Nine Steps to Emotional Freedom and I am continuing to answer the questions for truth, until I can say that,

"I am becoming a master of killing the fear of future failure or loss in my life that I am compulsively thinking about."

In Summary:

I have chosen to explore the feelings of unresolved fear, anger, worry & stress in Our Book Two because these feelings may generate unresolved pain & suffering in my life that I may compulsively think or worry about.

As human beings, none of us are perfect, so we have to learn how to stop our worrying about the unfair feelings, thoughts & images in our minds that is providing unfair thinking energy to our unresolved pain & suffering, unfair thinking energy that is keeping our worrying alive, until we learn what is creating the worrying process and we learn how to forgive ourselves & others, so we can start to kill this unresolved unfair pain & suffering that our worrying is keeping alive inside our conscious minds.

Once we do this, it will be easier for us to fully reconnect to our internal source of peace, joy, happiness & compassion that lives inside each of us. That is why I recommend that we use Positive Self-Talk to tell ourselves that our future lives will be fair to us and to tell us that there is no longer any need to worry.

I am repeating this positive self-talk mantra each day to stop my worrying, as needed,

"I am now protected from fear of future failure or loss by my conviction that my future life will fair to me."

How do I reduce the amount of worrying about my fear of future failure or loss that my memories, My Ego, or new events in my life may create inside my conscious mind? Q-160

# Chapter 4

## Killing the Unresolved Pain & Suffering in My Life

By killing the unresolved pain & suffering in my life, I am starting to live each day of my adult life with increasing passion, as I become able to fully reconnect to my internal source of love, peace, joy & compassion that I was born possessing and that I experienced each day of my life as a young child.

For many human beings, it is a frightening prospect to look inside their minds at their memories of the unresolved unfair pain & suffering that was created by the unfairness they experienced in their past lives. The fear of looking at this pain is the major reason why many human beings try to find joy & happiness in the external world, as far away from their internal pain & suffering as they can, so they do not have to look inside their minds for love & joy, because when do, they start to feel the unresolved pain & suffering that is living inside them.

Now that I am answering the questions for truth and I am practicing the Nine Steps to Emotional Freedom during each new day of my adult life, I am able to quickly kill any unresolved pain & suffering that may be generated inside my conscious mind by an unfair memory, My Ego or a new event in my life that will try to steal my joy & happiness from me.

Then, when my mind becomes free of this new pain & suffering, I am able to fully reconnect to my internal source of unconditional love which automatically fills my conscious mind with **continuous** love, peace, joy & compassion, as long as I continue practicing meditation & mindfulness to keep my mind clear of any new pain & suffering that may try to live inside my conscious mind in the future.

Now, I am able to choose the enjoyable feelings that I want to experience as I start to feel increasing passion for living during each new day of my life.

To help us to understand why so much unresolved pain & suffering is being created in our lives that prevents us from feeling continuous love, peace, joy & compassion, let us try to understand the lives of married adults who are trying to share love & joy with each other.

# Chapter 5

## Managing the Unfair Pain & Suffering that Kills a Marriage

The worry & stress in our adult lives increases the pain in our memories when we become married adults, when we do not know how to kill the unresolved unfair pain & suffering in our marriage because we have not learned how to forgive each other, such when the wife has difficulty forgiving the husband who has become a couch potato who watches sports on TV instead of supporting his wife with the love, compassion & support that she needs to help her complete the daily chores around the home, by helping her to take care of the children, such as, preparing their meals, cleaning their clothes, helping them with homework, helping them to understand the pain & unfairness that a childhood friend may create in their lives, or helping to support their desires for new childhood fun & adventures.

I could have used an example of a lazy & emotionally detached wife in a marriage, but I have never met one in my life experiences. In my experience, it has always been the husband not doing his fair share of the work or not providing enough emotional support to help make the marriage a success.

Even though there are lazy married women in the real world, I am not qualified to talk about them.

In my real life experience, as the years of marriage start to roll on by, the wife may start to feel unresolved pain each day of her married life whenever she starts reliving the unfair pain in her memories of how her husband has disappointed her so many times in the past, which Debra in the TV series, Everybody Loves Raymond expresses in words when she calls Raymond an "Idiot" whenever he is being insensitive to her needs for increased emotional support, or when she wants to talk to him about new disappointments in her life, or when her in-laws start to treat her unfairly again, or when she asks Raymond to help with the children or expresses her desire for some quiet personal privacy time so she can recharge her emotional batteries to help her prepare for the next new challenge in her life.

In real life, many husbands know they should be doing more work around the house to support their wives & family members and many of these husbands may grudgingly accept their wives' nagging whenever they start to feel their wives' pain & suffering which unfortunately, they may not know how to help their wives to resolve, especially when  they do not meet their wives' many expectations for making their married lives more successful, as the wisdom for a successful marriage says, " Help support your Loving Wife to enjoy A Happily Married Life".

Of course, a wife may no longer be motivated to meet a husband's expectations, either. As a result, the husband may start to feel that his wife no longer has romantic feelings for him because of all the unfair pain that he has created in her life, by letting her down so many times in the past.

Even so, like Debra, the wife may still love her husband and may continue to forgive him each day for not living up to her many expectations of him.

(Please refer to the Forgiving the Unresolved Pain & Suffering in My Life section in Chapter 3 of Our Book One)

**Disrespectful Comments about Married Life**

As result, in many marriages, like the one portrayed on TV by Debra & Raymond, a wife or husband may not be able to forgive themselves or their spouse for all the long term unfair pain & suffering in their marriages and as a result will file for divorce which is evidenced by 50 per cent of all real life marriages ending in divorce after 13 years in Canada, where I live. This occurs when the love & romance at the beginning of the marriage turns into a daily painful struggle for equality, respect, fairness, love & support.

Is it any wonder that a married couple may say:

"You can't live with them and you can't live without them"

"Those who can live alone & be happy are blessed."

Why is it difficult to generate ongoing support, fairness, romantic love & respect for a spouse's emotional needs inside a marriage?

## Disrespectful Comments by Wives about Their Husbands

The following fictional comments were made by married women who are being unfair & disrespectful to their husbands, as they express the unresolved pain that they feel about their marriages because they may not have learned how to fully forgive their husbands for the mistakes made in their marriages. To fully forgive they may need to reconnect to the full power of their internal unconditional love that is living inside them to help them generate powerful feelings of compassion & forgiveness for their husbands, especially when their husbands do not deserve forgiveness.

"After being married for a while, a husband and wife become two sides of a coin, they just can't face each other, but still they stay together.

The great question, which as a wife I have not been able to answer is, "What does a man want?

I had some words with my husband, and he had some paragraphs with me.

Some people ask the secret of our long marriage. The answer is we take the time, to go to a restaurant two times a week, for a candlelight dinner, soft music & dancing. He goes Tuesdays, I go Fridays.

I don't worry about terrorism. I was married for two years.

There's a way of transferring funds that is even faster than electronic banking. It's called marriage.

I've had bad luck with all my husbands. The first one left me and the second one didn't. The third gave me more children!

Two secrets to keep your marriage brimming. Whenever you're wrong, admit it and whenever you're right, shut up.

The most effective way to remember your husband's birthday is to forget it once.

You know what I did before I married? Anything I wanted to.

My husband and I were happy for twenty years. Then we met.

A good husband always forgives his wife when he's wrong.

Marriage is the only war where one sleeps with the enemy.

A woman inserted an ad in the classifieds, "Husband wanted". During the next few days she received a hundred letters. They all said the same thing, "You can have mine."

When another woman hurts you when she steals your husband, there is no better revenge than to let her keep him.

First Woman says proudly, "My husband's an angel!" Then the Second Woman says, "You're lucky, mine's still alive."

First there's the promise ring, then the engagement ring, then the wedding ring...and soon after....comes the Suffe... ring!" [84]

Married women who make comments, such as these, feel unresolved unfair pain in their marriages that they may not understand and may not know how to kill, so they make up these fictional comments to describe their suffering, to allow themselves some humor about being married.

And if you are a man, who is suffering from unresolved pain in your marriage, please change the gender from male to female in these comments, to help you feel some humor about being married.

Sometimes laughter, is the only relief we can obtain, when we do not know how to kill the unresolved unfair pain in our marriages, especially when we know that we are partially responsible for the unfair pain in our marriage, even though we may be trying our best, to forgive ourselves & our spouses and we may be trying to find ways to resolve our mutual pain, so we can replace it with increased sensitivity, understanding, love & forgiveness for one another.

## Increasing the Unresolved Suffering in a Marriage

Painful experiences often lead to increased unresolved pain in the marriage, when the needs of the husband & the wife are not being met. Eventually, when the pain in the marriage becomes greater than the love being shared and when the husband & wife are constantly fighting over who should be the boss in the marriage, the couple may give up trying to save their marriage and file for divorce.

Can I blame the wife for a failed marriage? Why?

Can I blame the husband for a failed marriage? Why?

No, I cannot blame either the wife or the husband when I realize, that both the husband & wife may be disconnected from their internal source of unconditional love when they do not understand how to kill the unresolved pain in their marriage and when they are not able to forgive each other. As a result, their marriage did not have much chance of success, from the very beginning on their wedding day.

## Why We Should Not Blame the Husband or the Wife

When a husband no longer feels unconditional love for his wife and he does not know how to kill the unresolved pain in the marriage, he may start ignoring his household duties because he wants to relax & do nothing, to allow all the unresolved pain from his marriage to be suppressed for a while, as he watches sports on TV, or works on one of his hobbies, or plays video games with the children. The husband knows that he should be more supportive of his wife & family, but he may not want any more stress in his life from his marriage, while he deals with the stress he has brought home from work or while he deals with the unresolved pain & suffering in his married life that he does not how to stop hurting him.

This leaves the wife doing more than her fair share of the household work, which is unfair, when she also works at a full time job during the day.

If the wife felt more unconditional love for her husband, it would be easier to forgive him, for not meeting her expectations and she would have more love, compassion & motivation to help train her man, to become a more supportive & loving husband.

**Training a Man to be a Good Husband**

In our industrialized society, many teenage boys are not trained to become nurturing members of their family, by learning to help around the house and by being supportive of other family members, when they are emotionally upset or physically not well. Boys are usually allowed to play sports and are allowed their privacy by parents who may not understand how to teach their children to resolve family disagreements by forgiving each other and by learning to kill the pain in their memories when there is worry, stress & unfairness in family situations.

Many parents do not know how to teach their teenage children to reconnect to the internal source of unconditional love of their childhood, or how to teach their children to forgive the parents for not being perfect mothers & fathers. If parents knew how to foster increased unconditional love & forgiveness in their children then their children would grow up to become teenagers who would still listen to a parent's advice. Then, the parents would be more willing to allow a teenager to make more decisions for themselves because they would trust them more. With more unconditional love & understanding, teenagers would be more willing to help around the home, and more importantly, they would know how to nurture family love by helping to resolve family arguments & misunderstandings.

In an unconditional loving family, each family member would use their love to unconditionally forgive other family members, to be able to kill the unresolved pain that is living in their minds, pain that started to live inside them when they had family arguments & disagreements.

In an unconditionally loving family, a teenager would share powerful love & respect with other family members and there would be no need for the parents to nag & complain when a child messes up at home or at school. This constant love & forgiveness inside the family would help resolve any family disputes that may occur.

In many dysfunctional families, nagging & complaining is used to try to revolve family disputes when family members do not know how to forgive each other. In these dysfunctional families there may only be a small amount of unconditional love being shared between family members and there may only be a small amount of willingness to help other family members as the family home life often becomes a battle ground, whenever someone is treated unfairly and new offers of help & advice are viewed as interference & meddling.

In contrast, in a healthy unconditional loving family there is nurturing family love that motivates all family members to do the work around the home that needs to be done, so that all family members will benefit, so that each family member is treated fairly and each family member is not asked to do more than their fair share of the work.

When a family member complains, then the family sits down together to resolve the dispute and offers forgiveness & unconditional love, especially when a family member is being treated unfairly by a parent or sibling.

When every family member helps with the chores around the home then the family has more free time, to play together as a family, as they enjoy the extra family time together, including family outings and playing games together. When they are together, family members express their unconditional love, understanding & sensitivity for each other, as they nurture family love with hugs & kisses and the words, "I love you".

In a healthy family, family members enjoy talking & playing with each other and no one offers advice to another family member unless it is asked for. An emotionally healthy family works well together when all the family members are connected to their internal source of unconditional love & forgiveness that they share with each other.

Unfortunately, many adult men who have been brought up in dysfunctional families may not have been taught family nurturing skills that can only be learned in a healthy family environment or from a loving mom, a loving father, a loving girlfriend or a loving wife.

And many men are not fully connected to their internal source of unconditional love & forgiveness, so they only have a small amount of love & forgiveness available to them when they become married, as they start to react to stressful marriage situations in the same way they did when they were teenagers, by becoming stressed out and wanting their privacy in front of the TV by becoming couch potatoes, or by leaving the home to play sports or go to social events with their male friends, or by working on their hobbies that do not include other stressful family members.

So, before the marriage falls apart, as 50 % of all marriages do today, it is crucial, that both the husband & wife learn how to fully reconnect to their internal source of peace, joy, happiness & compassion, so that they can use this powerful nurturing energy to forgive each other during stressful times in their married lives and they can use this powerful nurturing energy to show more love, understanding & sensitivity for each other.

Then, the husband will become more committed to doing what his wife asks him to do, to make the marriage more successful as he learns improved family nurturing skills that he may not have learned as a young child or as a rebellious teenager.

This is how the powerful nurturing energy of unconditional love can help many marriages to succeed when the marriage encounters stressful situations, by taking some of the burden away from the Super Mom who is trying to nurture children, maintain the house, work at a full time job during the day and still have the time & the energy left at the end of a long day to spend some private time with her husband, as they both try to nurture romantic love in their relationship as husband & wife. For couples without children, this is much easier.

In many marriages, the wife becomes the boss in the relationship, and many husbands are supportive of their wives being the boss, because the husband knows that his wife's family nurturing skills are superior to his and as long as she asks for his opinion and gives him his freedom to spend some quality time with his male friends, or allows him to work of his hobbies, then he will try to learn the family nurturing skills that he needs, to help make their marriage a success, when his wife is willing to forgive him whenever he makes mistakes or messes things up.

All men are rebels at heart and they will not always do what a wife tells a husband to do, even if doing so is in the best interests of their friends & family.

Statistically, the first six years of marriage becomes a battle to determine who is going to be the boss in the marriage.

"In many successful marriages, the smart man learns to make an agreement with his wife, that he will not give her any advice, unless she asks for it. The husband also agrees to allow the wife to give him advice whenever and as often as she wants to."

This is a paraphrase of President Jimmy Carter's words of wisdom, for the success in his marriage to Rosalind Carter, as he discussed the 60th anniversary of their marriage on the Tonight Show with J Leno on December 11, 2006

Many men require a lot of training before they become supportive husbands. Why?

To help is to understand why many men lack the nurturing skills needed for a success in a marriage, let us review the historical record of men over the last several thousand years so we can trace the evolution of family love and the evolution of social nurturing skills, from ancient times to the present day.

# Chapter 6

## The Evolution of Family & Social Nurturing Skills

My understanding of the history of nurturing unconditional love inside & outside the family, is based on my personal experience and the historical information I have gleaned from books & documentaries, such as The Natural History of Love by Morton Hunt.

Let me start by describing a fictional account of what may have happened in the days of the caveman over 50,000 years ago, when men & women learned to support each other, so they could nurture children and ensure the future well-being of the tribe. Please do not believe that this account is true because there is no historical evidence that social skills developed this way, but it is possible they may have.

The increasing family & social nurturing skills of women, may have occurred as women improved their ability to multitask, when women were left at home, back in the days of the caveman, to prepare the meals, clean the cave, make the clothes, gather vegetables & fruit growing in the wilderness, tend the sick & injured, and nurture the children.

Being put in charge of the family, while the men were away hunting, gave women the opportunity to improve their nurturing skills, and in doing so, women became superior to men. Women may have become masters at using their family nurturing skills as they learned to convince members of other families to work together, to get the chores done that were necessary for the survival of all the families & social groups living in the cave. Meanwhile, the men may have been out hunting in a cooperative effort to club big animals to death, to be able to bring home meat to the women in charge back at the cave.

Over thousands of years, the family & social skills of men & women would have improved, through the evolution of language, the discovery of fire, and the social interaction of men in clubbing all their rivals, to allow one of them to become chief of the local tribe.

Then one day, some brilliant person that I am guessing was a woman, discovered that when seeds taken from a plant where planted in a field, the family unit could start to enjoy a steady source of home grown food without having to wander throughout the land in search of game that could prove scarce. Their home grown food could also be gathered and stored to help feed domesticated animals that could become a source of food over the long cold winters.

Then, as the transition from hunter/gatherer to farmer/ landowner, slowly evolved, so did family & social nurturing skills evolve to meet the needs of the agricultural community of families who began living near each other on large plots of agricultural land that could support many separate families.

Later came the evolution from isolated agricultural farms, to villages, towns & countries, where the local men may have continued to play the game of politics & war, to determine who would be become king of the local tribes.

Meanwhile, the lady of the house may have been left back at home doing the majority of the work, while dear old hubby was out fighting his wars or playing political games, to help protect his family and their way of life back home, or so he claimed.

Up to this point in my fictional historical story of the evolution of family & social nurturing skills, there are no written records, so we can only surmise what actually occurred, based on the storytelling of shamans, who provided us with verbal accounts that were handed down from father to son & mother to daughter to help keep the oral traditions of the tribes & families alive. Such as the stories which have become legends as evidenced by Homer's tales told in the Iliad.

The most compelling story from ancient times is The Great Flood that enveloped the entire earth, a legend told by the ancient Greek philosopher Plato who said Atlantis was destroyed by a giant flood and earthquakes 9,000 years before the time of Solon, an Athenian statesmen. Solon lived in 600 BC which dates The Great Flood to 9,600 BC, which is 11,600 years ago

Researchers have found that such a great flood may have occurred as evidenced by ancient writings from all around the world, such as the story of Noah in the Christian Bible, and more importantly, as evidenced in our Earth's geological record when researchers found a 19 mile wide impact crater half a mile beneath a Greenland ice sheet, which provided scientists and archeologists with proof that a mile-wide meteorite impacted the planet's northern ice cap around 11,600 years ago.

This meteor impact may have melted the ice cap in the northern hemisphere, instantaneously creating great tidal waves that became The Great Flood, which ancient history tells us engulfed the entire surface of the Earth destroying any civilizations that existed at that time. This discovery supports a contentious theory proposed by researchers, including Graham Hancock and Dr. Robert Schoch, who believe that this cataclysmic impact may have wiped out the lost civilization of Atlantis that predates the accepted timeline of mainstream archeology.

In addition to this ancient mystery, no modern day researcher knows with certainty, when or how mankind learned to speak languages, cultivate plants, domesticate animals, or learned how to write, though many researchers are starting to believe that Atlantis was not the only great civilization that existed in Earth's far distant past, though we have very little evidence to support this theory.

Our written language only dates back a few thousand years, so the evidence of how men and women worked together to successfully raise children is largely unknown before that time except in myths & fables. The earliest known form of writing is the Sumerian cuneiform language found on clay tablets that date back to 3,400 BC which is older than the Egyptian Hieroglyphics language.

What I have been able to learn from these ancient writings and from modern day researchers is that historically, the main provider & protector of the family was the man who demanded that he should be the boss of the family, in social interactions with other families or with representatives of the king, including the tax collectors and other administrative officials. The world outside the home became a man's world, where women were marginalized and kept largely in bondage at home, subservient to the man of the house.

This was not entirely true for aristocratic women who had servants and who were allowed to use their social nurturing skills to entertain the nobles from other families & other lands. Even so, noble men still ruled and sold off their daughters in arranged marriages to consolidate or expand the power of the family or the kingdom. That is why by the 16th century, many of the kings & queens of Europe, were interrelated by blood through arranged marriages that had been going on for hundreds of years.

Meanwhile back at home, the average woman in the realm was still being treated in a subservient way by her husband. A man loved his family but still felt superior to his wife and demanded to be the boss, the final arbitrator & the final decision maker in any family discussion or decision. And what could the poor wife do in this situation, when through an arranged marriage she was stuck with a man who, as her husband, may not have respected her decision making skills in social situations where other men were involved.

The alternatives open to her were few & bleak. She could ask her parents if she could move back home with the children. In many countries this was against the law. If she tried to escape on her own, the husband had the right to take away the children. What could the average wife do when she did not have money and when she was treated as a social outcast, if she tried to live on her own? The only viable escape for a woman besides running away from a potential bad marriage was to join a convent of nuns and give her life to the church.

It was not until the industrial revolution that women gained the opportunity to become financially independent of men. This financial independence slowly grew, over the last 300 hundred years in industrialized countries, to the point where women began to use their growing financial independence & superior social nurturing skills to start demanding a voice in how their country should be run.

In the last two hundred years, men started to realize that if they wanted to have a successful marriage, they would have to change their attitudes and start accepting the demands of their wives for more say in community decision making activities such as the election of local officials for the town council, even though women had no right to vote in elections or run for office.

In the meantime, women with their increased financial independence were demanding more decision making power in resolving family disputes and in the family financial decision making. Also, women started to use their financial independence to rally for changes to the common law of the land to obtain custody of the children in the event of a divorce. A hundred years ago, very few women divorced their husbands. Morally & socially it was not accepted and when it happened the woman was usually the one blamed.

Meanwhile back at home, wives & daughters started to demand more respect from the men in their lives. Men soon found out that in our industrialized society, the average woman would no longer accept an arranged marriage. It is not surprising that The Age of Romantic Love only started after the industrial revolution had empowered women financially and had provided the common people with enough money to establish the new lower & middle classes in our industrialized society. This allowed single adults of the common working class in industrialized nations to have enough social time, when men & women no longer had to work seven days a week to earn a wage, to practice the new art of romance, as they found the spare time to learn singing, dancing, how to play musical instruments & how to write poetry, in an attempt to woo the ideal lover who had previously only lived in their dreams.

Prior to this, the poems & stories of romance were written by the aristocracy who were the only ones to have sufficient money & enough leisure time to practice the art of courting a lover with offers of social intrigue & romance, which allowed a woman to choose the man she wanted to marry, even though arranged marriages were still being used to secure financial & political influence between families.

When The Age of Romantic Love began during the Industrial Revolution, the average lower & middle class woman realized she was superior to many men, in family & social nurturing skills and so the average woman began to use her skills to rally other women to social causes which supported improved laws & community financing to help impoverished families and destitute children.

With their new financial power and their superior social nurturing skills, women started to organize into political lobby groups and started demanding equal rights under the law. After much social discourse & political rallies by women to demand a change in the laws, the last bastions of male supremacy began to fall 100 + years ago, after women acquired the right to vote, in local & national elections, and to push for laws to enhance the rights of women & children, so they could enjoy the same equality & fairness under the law, as men.

Even in present day marriages, the husband who has wooed and successfully married the woman of his dreams, is still at a big disadvantage, when it comes to family & social nurturing skills. Many men still find it difficult to emotionally open their hearts and discuss their problems with their wives. And many men have not learned how to nurture emotional support by discussing their personal issues with other men. Women, on the other hand, continue to rally around each other for mutual support as they discuss family & social nurturing issues, especially concerning their children & husbands and their extended family of parents & relatives.

Men have much to learn from women, about family & social nurturing skills, to be able to openly discuss personal & family issues that require men to become emotionally open & vulnerable when discussing their private lives. This is not easy for many men to learn.

For example, in our industrialized societies today, many boys are still being brought up to compete with other boys in sports and this training for competition continues as boys become men, who compete with each other in business. Men learn to treat other men as potential adversaries as they compete with other men to win jobs & build successful businesses, as they learn to not discuss any family or social issues with other men that could give their competition an advantage.

Is it any wonder that many men are reluctant to talk about family & social nurturing issues that are affecting their married lives, when these men are from dysfunctional families, where superior family & social nurturing skills were not taught to them as children?

Are any men in your personal life starting to show increasing emotional openness, compassion, tenderness & sensitivity in a family or social relationship? If so, why?

**How Men are Improving Their Family Nurturing Skills**

I predict that the qualities of emotional openness, compassion, tenderness & sensitivity will become the norm when adult men start to fully reconnect to their internal source of unconditional love and learn to be emotionally open with other men, when historically, men have been treating each other as potential adversaries that they may have to compete with someday to obtain a share of the scarce resources in the world, such as money, better jobs, promotions and girlfriends, etc.

Currently, many husbands do not have the proven ability to nurture unconditional love with the understanding & skill of their wives, especially when a wife leaves the family tasks to her husband, while she is away from the family home for a week or more.

A typical modern day husband may find assuming the roles of wife & mother, difficult to do, when he is left at home alone with the children for a week or more. When the husband agrees to do all the housework and meet the family social commitments for the week, he may find that he is in trouble when he does not know what to do because of his lack of superior family nurturing skills. This includes the family nurturing skills required to help the children to resolve any problems at school or to help the children to forgive each other during family disputes, as the husband tries to successfully motivate the children to live together peacefully by sharing love & forgiveness with each other, as he tries to help them to navigate through their social activities after school such as drama clubs & going to birthday parties, as he helps the children to wake up, get out of bed, eat breakfast & get ready for school each day. Then, as he washes the children's clothes, becomes the referee in family arguments, pick the kids up after school, makes the dinners, washes the dishes, plays with the children, answers their many questions in the evening, referees their games & playtime, gets the kids ready for bed, say prayers with the children, reads them bedtime stories, etc.

Need I go on about many married men lacking adequate social nurturing skills? How about, planning activities for the family to do on the weekends, holidays, at birthday parties & family dinners, when the in-laws are invited over. How about, buying new clothes for the children, and of course most importantly for the husband, how about the task of caring for Hubby, which he will not get when his loving wife is away for a week or more.

By the time the wife gets home, the supposedly superior man about the house will have new respect for the woman he married. And "Yes" go on and say it. She has earned the title many times over.

She is Super Mom! in a typical modern family where her husband is not doing his fair share of the work around the family home.

And for the next week or so, Hubby will be probably be on his best behavior around the house as he tries extra hard to support his wife.

Unfortunately after a few weeks, his thousands of years of genetic & historical pre-programming will probably start to take over again, as his wife tells him, once again, that he forgot to take out the garbage. So, he utters a sigh of resignation as he gets up off the couch to do his job. He has once again become the lazy couch potato.

As husbands, we are fortunate to have wives who are willing to put up with us because our wives are willing to sacrifice their time, their efforts, their money and unfortunately sometimes their health, to take care of their families with their superior family & social nurturing skills that they have been perfecting for thousands of years.

As I investigated the historical evolution of family & social nurturing skills and then compared this historical evidence to my own personal experience with the married couples that I know, I have concluded that a woman's unconditional love for her family, her multitasking skills & her family & social nurturing skills are superior to many men, that I know, including mine. The social nurturing skills of many men are limited due to lack of proper training during childhood, as we learned to face new challenges in the competitive arena of life, to beat our foes and to become the victor, as we have been learning to do for thousands of years. As men, we have been trained to take home the rewards of our success so we can help provide for our families, as we use our limited family nurturing skills to help family members to share family love and enjoy fun & adventures together as a family.

As a husband, in an effort to help maintain the existing status quo for a few more years, I have decided to give up my largely imaginary role as the head of the family. It belongs to someone, who has superior family multitasking skills, better family communications skills & better family & social nurturing skills than me. Yes, you got it. It is my lovely wife Linda, who knew what I was like before she married me. But for some unknown reason, which will probably remain a mystery to me, she decided to take pity on me in the belief that she could help me to become a supportive husband and so she agreed to marry me in a moment of romantic weakness. After many years of marriage, she has not given up trying to mold me into a superior nurturing & loving husband.

However, today's young marriageable women are setting the standards higher for the men that they are willing to marry. So in the future, the era of the man as a coach potato is drawing to a close.

**Killing All The Unresolved Pain & Suffering in a Marriage**

My example of the couple who chose to get a divorce describes a typical marriage in today's world, where the partners in the marriage have limited access to their source of unconditional love & true friendship and who may not have learned how to kill the unresolved pain & suffering that is living inside their memories of the many disappointments their partner has created in their marriage.

(Please refer to the Forgiving Others Who Do Not Deserve Forgiveness section in Chapter 3 of Our Book One)

Unless married couples become able to fully reconnect to their internal source of unconditional love to generate powerful compassion & forgiveness for each other so they can romantically fall in love with each other, once again, the years of unresolved lingering disappointments in the marriage may doom them to eventual failure & divorce.

Fortunately for me, I married a wonderful woman who is very forgiving when I mess up. I have been truly blessed as a husband and I pray that in the future my loving wife will continue to allow me the privilege of being her husband with my many faults.

Unfortunately, 50% of married couples are divorced after 13 years of marriage in Canada and by the time the remaining 50 % who stay married are in their forties, 20% of these couples are no longer sleeping together because they do not know how to forgive each other for the unresolved pain & suffering that they have created in their marriage, as this unfair pain & suffering blocks their desire for intimacy, romance & sex.

This statistic leaves a only a 40% chance that my marriage will last forever, a marriage where my loving wife has learned to forgive me at least a couple of times a week when I continue to mess up and create small unintentional disappointments in her life.

And fortunately, she has been able to forgive me for any major pain & suffering that I have created in her life because her unconditional love for me is powerful enough to generate the forgiveness in her heart that she needs to kill the unresolved pain & suffering in her life that I created, for which I do not deserve forgiveness.

So to help me to mess up less often in our future married life, I am answering the questions for truth that I have modified to apply them to my life, such as,

How can I foster romantic love in my marriage when I look at my spouse and automatically start to feel the unresolved pain & suffering, which I may blame myself or my spouse for creating in our marriage?

And how do we kill this unresolved pain & suffering in our marriage?

And to help you to understand this marital wisdom please ask yourself these questions to help understand why most marriages fail and why few (40% or less) succeed in fostering long term romantic love inside the marriage,

How many successful long term marriages do you know of, in your personal life experience, where you have observed a married couple who are still romantically in love with one another and who share abundant laughter & enjoyment with each other, when they are sharing fun & adventures with friends & family?

How many failed marriages, do you know of in your personal life experience where you intimately know at least one of the couples involved and you have personally observed how their unresolved pain & suffering grew during the years of married life, when they did not know how to forgive each other, as they slowly lost their powerful romantic love for each other and as their disappointments with each other begin to accumulate inside their marriage, which eventually led to irreconcilable differences that ended in their divorce?

Reconciliation between two partners in a marriage is possible when a couple is able to fully reconnect to their childhood source of unconditional love that automatically generates strong feelings of love & compassion for each other, as they use this powerful energy of love to forgive each other. This is how my wife & I have learned to make our marriage an ongoing success, as we share hugs & kisses each day, as we talk about the trials & tribulations of the day, as we share our intimacy & our love to navigate through each new day's adventures that can generate new fun into our lives or can generate new unresolved pain in our lives that we have to learn how to kill with forgiveness to keep our marriage an ongoing success.

When we are successful at killing any new unresolved pain & suffering that may enter our marriage, we have the opportunity to fall romantically in love, once again, as we use our childhood abilities to share powerful unconditional love & forgiveness with each other, as long as we are able to kill the new unresolved pain & suffering that may temporally block our ability to feel romantic love for each other.

How can we help men to improve their qualities of emotional openness, compassion, tenderness & sensitivity, in family & social relationships? Q-161

**Supporting Our Future Children**

Hopefully, we will be able to teach this wisdom for a successful marriage to the children in our extended family of friends & relatives when they ask for help, so we can help the children to remain fully connected to the unconditional love of their childhood, as they grow up to become teenagers. We taught this wisdom to our son who will hopefully become a role model for our grandchildren, who in turn, will pass their childhood wisdom for sharing unconditional & nurturing true friendship to our great grandchildren, someday in the distant future.

Then, when these future children grow into adults, this powerful unconditional love will help support their marriages that will be created by two mentally healthy human beings who possess the powerful unconditional love of their childhood to share equally in the decision making and the work required to increase the shared love & the benefits of being married. The divorce rate should come way down from its current 50 % level today as this dream of ours becomes a reality, as future married couples learn how to kill any new unresolved pain & suffering that may enter into their marriage by learning how to forgive each other, especially when one of the partners does not deserve forgiveness, as they share increasing love & forgiveness with each other and with their children & their extended friends & family. This sounds like utopia on Earth to me.

How do I nurture the sharing of love & joy in my relationships, without also generating unintentional pain & suffering? Q-162

## How a Man Can Re-Energize His Marriage

I am hoping that married men will start using The Wisdom of Children to become able to express genuine love for their wives, in their own words, such as these,

"You are the love of my life and I am very fortunate to be your husband.

Thank you for all your ongoing love & support.

Now that I am a little wiser than I was when you married me, I am trying to kill the major unfair pain & suffering in my life that is hiding my ability to love you more passionately, because I want to use this increased love to become more supportive & considerate of your desires & needs.

And thank you for the forgiveness that you keep offering me, when I continue to mess up, as you keep trying to help me become a more loving & nurturing husband & father.

I deeply & sincerely apologize for not living up to your expectations of me and I promise to be more supportive in the future."

Words, such as these, will help re-energize the love that a wife has for her husband, when she looks into his eyes and knows that these words are coming from the pure unconditional love in her husband's heart. Many marriages could be saved with words such as these, as long as the husband starts to back up his words with more loving deeds, more understanding, more openness to new ideas and the increased sensitivity, tenderness, trust, compassion & forgiveness that will nurture their marriage & their friends & family.

To be successful, a husband needs to fully reconnect to his childhood internal source of unconditional love to become able to generate the powerful motivation & passion that he needs, to fully support his wife & family and to start meeting more of his wife's expectations by doing what his wife asks him to do, as soon as she asks him to do it, when her expectations & her superior nurturing skills are in the best interests of their marriage & their family.

# Chapter 7

## My Separated Nature

By the time I became an adult, before I married the love of my life, I had become a separated person as I started to mistakenly believe that there is an external reality that lives separately from my mind & body. I felt separate from all the life in this external reality because I had disconnected myself from my internal childhood source of peace, joy, happiness & compassion that I was born possessing.

As a separated person I started to live my life inside out, by falsely conceiving of me as "I am separate" from the world. And I hoped that the external world contained a source of continuous joy & happiness that I could acquire for my life because I had stopped trying to find joy & happiness inside of me in my internal world.

As I tried to manipulate the external world to obtain joy & happiness, I began to realize that other people are controlling the scarce resources of external joy & happiness.

As I result, I began to feel anxiety & fear of failure due to not being in control of my external joy & happiness and due to the prospect that I may never be able to rest in peace because I may be unable to obtain a secure source of lasting joy & happiness in the external world.

Fortunately for me, my lack of success in the external world motivated me to realize that I had made a mistake, when I started to look for a secure continuous source of joy & happiness in the external world, long after I had disconnected myself from my internal childhood source of joy & happiness because I was afraid to look inside my mind at the thousands of memories of unfair pain & suffering that I had accumulated in my life from my childhood until now, memories that I did not know how to stop hurting me whenever I started to relive one of them in my daily life and that I did not know how to kill, especially the painful memory of the unfairness of my mother's death.

I began to realize that my lack of success at finding continuous joy & happiness in the external world was motivating me, to try once again, to regain control over my ability to fully reconnect to my internal childhood source of unconditional love that I felt when I was a child. I realized that I must be willing to face the painful memories that I automatically felt when I started to look inside my mind, whenever I tried to find an internal source of the powerful unconditional love that I wanted in my life. I realized that only by looking inside my conscious mind did I have a chance to fully reconnect to my internal childhood source of joy & happiness, to become able to access the continuous stream of unconditional love that I was born possessing & that I was always connected to when I was a child, a connection that I had lost by the time I became an adult.

Fortunately, many of my memories of the powerful unconditional love of my childhood were proof to me that my childhood experiences were real, so I asked the question,

How do I fully reconnect to the internal source of love, peace, joy & compassion of my childhood, so I can start to feel & then share this powerful unconditional love with all the life that is surrounding me, especially with my friends & family? Q-17

(Please refer to the Question Q-17 in the Learning to Understand My True Self section in Chapter 6 of Our Book One)

To help me to accelerate the process of reconnection to my internal childhood source of love, I studied the wisdom of the sages who were able to live their adult lives in a state of continuous unconditional love. It took me more than ten years as I used their wisdom to learn how to kill all the major unresolved pain & suffering in my conscious mind.

To  start killing the major unfair pain in my conscious mind, I learned to stop feeding my memories the unfair thinking energy that my unfair pain needed to stay alive inside my conscious mind, to start clearing the unfair pain from the pathway to my internal source of joy & happiness, as I learned that I could start to rest in peace, as I began to feel increasing unconditional love in my life each day, as the major unfair pain in my conscious mind started dying due to lack of unfair thinking energy and then disappeared from my conscious mind when it had no energy left to stay alive inside my mind.

When my unresolved pain & suffering was gone from my conscious mind, I stopped being a separated person as I became fully reconnected to my internal source of unconditional love.

Then, I decided to write Our Book with the help of my son, to help me distill the wisdom of the unconditional love of children that lived in my heart, so I could help my future grandchildren. And now I want to help our friends & family and you the reader of Our Book to become able to share this powerful unconditional love & forgiveness with your families & friends.

How did I become a separated person? Q-163

**Why do I Sometimes Feel like an Idiot**

Why do I sometimes feel like an idiot when I know that if had answered the questions for truth I would **not** have treated myself or someone else, so unfairly?

Why did I start disconnecting from my internal source of joy & happiness so many years ago?

When I was a child, why didn't my parents teach me how to stay fully connected to my internal source of love for all life that I was born possessing?

The answers to these questions is obvious when I look back on my life. My parents did not know how to fully reconnect to their internal source of joy & happiness and could not teach me how to kill the unresolved pain & suffering in my memories that was slowly disconnecting me from my internal childhood source of love, peace, joy & compassion, as I accumulated more & more unfair painful memories as I grew up. There is nothing to forgive. My parents did the best they could. They loved me, nurtured me and tried to help me to become a wonderful human being with superior social & family nurturing skills.

By the time I became an adult, I had lost my connection to my internal childhood source of unconditional love. Then, I spent many years of struggle & suffered many disappointments as I tried to find it again, so I could start to fully reconnect with my powerful source of unconditional love.

Many years have gone by, since the beginning of my quest to experience continuous love in my adult life, by learning how to fully reconnect to my internal source of unconditional love, so I could kill all the major unfair pain from my memories that was blocking my connection to this childhood source of love.

Now, I am using my childhood feelings of love in my adult life, at a fast fun filled rate, to help to improve & evolve as a human being who is trying to share increasing unconditional love with my friends & family, as I continue to fulfill the dream my parents have for me, which is to fully enjoy life and be happy.

I know my parents are proud of my brother & me, as I keep the memories of my parents alive inside my mind and as I dream that their spirits are still alive, as they enjoy new fun & adventures in heaven.

Unfortunately, my mother died when I was young and she did not live long enough to savor the success of her children, or enjoy the birth of her grandchildren and my father died a few years after his retirement, so he only had a few years to love & nurture the grandchildren that he adored.

The power of my internal childhood source of unconditional love continues to generate intense love for my parents each day of my adult life, as I continue to spiritually thank my parents for helping to mold me into the man that I have become today. And I am grateful for the love & support that I have received from my wife, my son & our friends & family.

This powerful love lives in my heart, alongside the memories of my wonderful childhood & the love for my parents, memories that are helping to motivate me to continuing writing books of wisdom for sharing unconditional love & nurturing true friendship with everyone in our lives.

# Chapter 8

## The Golden Rule of Conduct

It is unconditional love that has inspired mankind since ancient times to adopt the Golden Rule of Conduct as an ethical code that states,

"Every Human Being on Earth has a right to fair treatment and a responsibility to ensure fairness, honesty, respect & justice for others." [85]

Justice refers to being treated honestly and fairly under the laws of the land. And in many countries such as the United States, justice requires fair & respectful treatment under the law for all citizens of the country, without discrimination as to race, color or creed, including different religious beliefs.

I believe that the unconditional love living inside the hearts of all human beings has inspired our ancestors to live by the Golden Rule of Conduct for centuries in their effort to treat all human beings with unconditional love, fairness, & respect. My belief is based on the evidence that unconditional love is the basis of all fair & just social interaction between human beings, as shown by mankind's answers to the meaning & purpose of our lives that we have been seeking answers to for thousands of years.

This understanding of the human condition that we share unites all human beings on this planet by the Golden Rule of Conduct that we are all born possessing and which we experience as our internal universal connection to unconditional love that motivates us from childhood to adulthood to protect all life and to treat all human beings with unconditional love, fairness, & respect.

This is evidenced by the universal acceptance of The Golden Rule of Conduct by the major world Religions [88]

Christianity                Thou shalt love thy neighbor as thyself –

Bible - Matthew 22:39

Do to others as you would have them do to you – Bible - Luke 6:31

| | |
|---|---|
| Confucianism | Do not do to others what you would not like yourself. Then there will be no resentment against you, either in the family or in the state. - Analects 12:2 |
| Hinduism | This is the sum of duty; do naught onto others what you would not have them do unto you. - Mahabharata 5,1517 |
| Islam | No one of you is a believer until he desires for his brother that which he desires for himself. – Sunnah |
| Judaism | What is hateful to you, do not do to your fellowman. This is the entire Law; all the rest is commentary. - Talmud, Shabbat 3id |
| Taoism | Regard your neighbor's gain as your gain, and your neighbor's loss as your own loss. – Tai Shang Kan Yin P'ien |
| Zoroastrianism | That nature alone is good which refrains from doing another whatsoever is not good for itself. - Dadisten-I-dinik, 94,5 |

The Golden Rule of Conduct is also accepted by the Buddhist religion which excludes a discussion on a belief in God to concentrate on an understanding of The Science of The Mind which is based on the desire to understand our human nature & our existence as unconditionally loving human beings.

**My Buddha Nature**

Buddhists believe in spiritual beings, who love and support us. For example, Thich Nhat Hanh in his book, Buddha Mind, Buddha Body, describes our spiritual Buddha nature that lives inside each of us, when he says,

"There is a Buddha in you. It is called the Buddha nature, the capacity of being aware of what is going on." [89]

And "If you find yourself in some difficulty, step aside and allow the Buddha to take your place. The Buddha is in you. This works in all situations." [90]

The spiritual ability of Buddha & God that lives inside us, helps us to live as unconditionally loving spiritual beings inside human bodies on Our Precious Mother Earth.

A Buddhist may say that there are many differences between my concept of a Christian God and his concept of the Buddha. This is absolutely true. However, I hope that we can reach an agreement that both Buddha and God share the same desire for all human beings to share unconditional love & nurture true friendship with everyone on Our Precious Mother Earth.

Based on my Christian understanding of God, I believe that when I die My Soul will be born again in a new body in Heaven.

Whereas a Buddhist believes that his spiritual essence will be reincarnated in a new body on Earth or some other planet.

 Thich Nhat Hanh describes the mind as eternal when he says, "In the Buddhist teaching because mind is not local it cannot die, it can only transform." [91]

And he teaches us that our mind was not born and will not die. However our mind is not permanent, it is always changing as he teaches us that nothing remains permanent, everything changes, though nothing is lost, it is only transformed.

Please read the book Buddha Mind, Buddha Body by Thich Nhat Hanh to explore the Buddhist concepts of no birth, no death, Interdependence & Impermanence and The Buddhist Science of The Mind. This book is based on a desire to understand our human nature as we try to live in the real world which offers us the potential for living a wonderful life on Earth that is filled with joy & happiness and this book helps us to understand why we have a tendency to delude ourselves as human beings, whenever we are distracted by our negative desires that try to convince us to live in a make believe delusional world that creates pain & suffering in our lives.

Thich Nhat Hanh helps us to live without distractions or delusions as we study the wisdom of Buddha that he has proven to be true in his life experiences as a Buddhist when he learned how to live in a continuous state of unconditional love, true friendship & Non Violence.

This is why Thich Nhat Hanh was nominated for the 1967 Nobel Peace Prize by Dr Martin Luther King Jr, the American civil rights activist. Thich Nhat Hanh's life became an inspiration to me as I read about his efforts to end the armed conflict & suffering during the Vietnam war and to help the boat people who tried to flee Vietnam, as he advocated love, forgiveness & non-violent action by living in a state of continuous love, peace, joy & compassion to become able to live in harmony with all sentient life, especially with all human beings on Our Precious Mother Earth.

The Buddhist tradition of Non Violence follows the Golden Rule of Conduct which has been practiced by Buddhists for thousands of years and which has been adopted by great leaders such as Mahatma Gandhi, the political & spiritual leader of India during the Indian independence movement and Martin Luther King Jr as a leader of the civil rights movement in the United States.

Buddhism    Hurt not others in ways that you yourself would find hurtful. - Udana-Varga 5,1

Buddhist wisdom is the result of a 2500 year quest to understand The Science of The Mind to help all human beings on Our Precious Mother Earth to understand how our minds should work, so we can use this wisdom to help us kill any unresolved pain & suffering in our lives that may diminishing our ability to share unconditional love & forgiveness with other human beings.

Buddhism spiritually unites everyone who tries to understand and use The Science of The Mind to practice non-violence and to help nurture & protect all life on Earth.

This truth of the wide spread use of the Golden Rule is evidence that our internal childhood source of unconditional love has motivated all races & all cultures on our planet for thousands of years to help nurture, protect & love all human beings on Earth as spiritual brothers & sisters.

However, this is not proof that all human beings have inside them, a childhood source of universal unconditional love & compassion, a desire for true friendship and a sense of belonging, as members of a universal family of all human beings who live on Earth.

You have to prove that The Golden Rule is true in your own experience, by observing this principle of non-violent conduct among other human beings as you observe it working in the lives of your friends, family & neighbors, as they show compassion for each other.

And when you understand this principle of unconditional love, you will realize that human beings who treat others with anger, violence, abuse, contempt, lying, stealing, rape & murder, do so when they are disconnected from their Internal Childhood Source of Unconditional Love for all the life that surrounds them.

To encourage you to observe this principle working in your own life, I have shown you how the universal adoption of The Golden Rule of Conduct by the religions of the world over the last several thousand years provides evidence that we are all born with a capacity for unconditional love that inspires us to relate to other human beings with love, compassion, forgiveness, tolerance, honesty, justice, fairness & respect.

## What does Fairness & Unfairness in Life mean to me?

When I think about the fair & unfair experiences in my life, I am able to use my Free Will to decide whether or not to apply The Golden Rule of Conduct to 100% of my life experiences as a guiding principle that I can use to help me understand my friends, my family & my neighbors, even though I may not want to apply this rule of conduct to other people in my life, such as business associates, strangers, people of a different political party, culture, or faith who I may sometimes desire to treat with unfairness, dishonesty & disrespect when I do not agree with their beliefs or behavior, especially when they treat me unfairly.

Fairness in my life occurs when I am treated with unconditional love, compassion, forgiveness, honesty & respect and an offer of true friendship, by another human being.

And I create fairness in my life by treating other human beings with unconditional love, honesty & respect which generates positive consequences in my future according to The Law of Karma.

Unfairness in my life occurs when I am treated with dishonesty, disrespect, rejection, indifference, or hostility by another human being.

And I create ongoing unfairness in my life when I feed unfair thinking energy to the unfair pain that is being generated by my negative memories of the unfair experiences in my past life, energy which keeps this unfair pain alive & active in my conscious mind.

## The Law of Karma

"The Law of Karma ensures that another person will be fairly punished, when he hurts me unfairly, by manipulating me, by lying to me, by stealing from me, or by verbally or physically abusing me. I may not punish him but he will still suffer for his hurtful actions, because the Law of Karma states that a person always experiences the fair consequences of his actions. If his actions are good the consequences will be good later in his life. If his actions are bad then he will be punished in full measure for the hurt that he has caused.

I have Faith that the Law of Karma works based on my life experiences that have shown me that it is working to ensure fairness, in my life and in the lives of all human beings that I know."

(Please refer to The Buddhist Law of Karma section in Chapter 23 of Our Book One)

Will I make the commitment to treat every human being that I know, associate with, or meet for the first time, with fairness, honesty & respect, according to The Golden Rule of Conduct?

**Reconnecting to Unconditional Love**

I am Practicing The Wisdom of Children to become able to enhance my connection to My Internal Childhood Source of Unconditional Love which enables me to practice The Golden Rule of Conduct.

I have asked the children in my adult life to teach me how to enhance my connection to the unconditional love of my childhood, by observing them as they enjoy their childhood while playing with other children or by asking their parents for help in understanding why their children feel intense passion for enjoying all that life has to offer them, especially their desire for new fun & adventures in their lives.

All children live in the state of continuous unconditional love that they are born possessing, which is their natural state of being. Young children are overflowing with unconditional love for all the life around them. It is unfortunate that many of us lose our internal connection to this unconditional love by the time we become adults. It is still inside us, buried under all our memories of the unresolved pain & suffering that we experienced growing up. To fully reconnect to our internal childhood source of unconditional love, we need to learn how to kill the unfair pain in our memories that is preventing us from fully experiencing the love, peace, joy & compassion that is being continuously generated by our internal childhood source of unconditional love, which we cannot always feel when it is being blocked by the sprouted memory seeds of the unfair suffering that is contained in our painful memories that we may be reliving each day of our adult lives, pain energy that is stored in The Room of Memories in our subconscious minds.

As we practice The Wisdom of The Children we become able to kill all the major unfair pain in our memories, to stop it blocking the pathway to our internal love, to become able to fully reconnect to our powerful unconditional love for all the life on Our Precious Mother Earth that lives inside us, especially our powerful love for our friends & family that we felt when we were young children.

**The Role of Unconditional Love**

To fully reconnect to my internal childhood source of unconditional love I am asking this question,

How do I relive my childhood memories of unconditional love? Q-167

To experience powerful feelings of love, peace, joy & compassion in my adult life, I am remembering what it was like to be a child. Unconditional love is my natural state of being that I was born possessing as a baby. To fully reconnect with this internal childhood source of unconditional love, I am learning to relive my memories of when I was very young. These memories contain the wisdom of how I can fully reconnect to my internal childhood source of peace, joy, happiness & compassion as an adult that will provide me with the increased motivational energy that I need to help accomplish my goals each day as I become more successful in life and as I begin to share this increasing love & forgiveness in my life with my friends & family.

When I am fortunate enough to be the parent or guardian of a young child, then I can ask the child to help me to awaken my childhood memories of unconditional love, by teaching me how to become a child again, by playing children's games and by sharing make believe childhood fantasy worlds with young children. As I share the children's play time, I am observing how the children love all life unconditionally, as the children play together. Then, I try to remember the details of how I felt when I was a young child when I shared unconditional love with all the life around me, especially with my friends & family. This process of becoming a child again, helps me to reconnect to my childhood memories of unconditional love.

And when I am not fortunate enough to be a parent or guardian of a young child, than I can go to a playground and ask a parent who is there protecting the children, for permission to observe the unconditional love of the children who are playing there. I can bring along a copy of Our Book Two to explain to the parent what I are trying to do, which is to use my perception of the unconditional love being shown by the children in the playground to help me to relive my memories of the universal unconditional love that I experienced as a young child.

As I watch the children and pretend that I am one of them, I will begin to experience the children's unconditional love for playing, because they are fully connected to the power of their love that is emanating from all the life in the universe, a love that is surrounding them in the playground. Then, as I begin enjoying the experience of pure unconditional love emanating from the children at play, I will begin to realize that they are not separate from me. I am connecting to each child in the playground by this universal love peace, joy & compassion that the young children are sharing with all sentient life around them, which includes me, as they see me sitting beside their parent or the guardian who is protecting them.

In this way, I become united with these children inside one big universal family of human beings who are trying to share unconditional love with each other, as we become spiritual brothers & sisters, who are learning as adults to share our rediscovered childhood unconditional love & compassion for each other, as we learn to play like children, once again, in our adult lives.

Then, I may begin to realize that the energy strings of The Primordial Awareness of My Mind are connecting me to all the life that is surrounding me, including all the children in the playground, as these energy strings begin connecting me to the memories of my unconditional love, when I was a child.

Whenever I watch young children at a playground, I begin to realize this experience of re-connecting to all the life in the universe, lives deep inside me and I begin to realize that I was born possessing this universal love for all life and that I never truly lost this love as I grew up. Its source was only hidden from me by the time I became an adult by the unresolved pain & suffering that I was accumulating in my mind as I grew from a childhood into adulthood.

My reconnection to the internal childhood source of this unconditional love may at first be a fleeting experience that does not last long. Then, as I begin to look at all the life around me, at the sun, the sky, the flowers, the experience of laughter & the love of the children playing, my unconditional love for all the life around me will start to grow until it demands my conscious mind's full attention, as I begin to experience my connection to all life in the universe, as I begin to fully reconnect my mind & body to my internal childhood source of unconditional love for all this life.

When I achieve success at reconnecting to this powerful unconditional love for longer periods each day, my life only gets better each day, as I experience more unconditional love, peace, joy & compassion in my daily life that I can share with my friends & family. My connection to all the life surrounding me starts to live inside me continuously, as I start to feel the primordial energy strings of the universe fully reconnecting me to the unconditional love emanating from the life in the universe. Then, I begin sharing a giving & taking relationship with all this life that I am universally connected to, by the energy strings of the universe that are powering all the atoms in my body and powering the thinking & feeling energy inside my conscious mind.

(Please refer to The Energy Strings of The Universe section in Chapter 22 of Our Book One)

# Chapter 9

## My Compassionate Watcher

As I experience unconditional love, I realize that I am an observer of life as I sit inside my mind and watch my feelings, thoughts & images as they enter my mind, stay for a while, and then disappear from my mind.

I call the observer of the activities of my mind by the name My Compassionate Watcher, who I refer to every time I say the words "I am".

My Compassionate Watcher helps me to use meditation to connect me to the vast spiritual energy field of the universe that is motivating me to experience continuous spiritual love, peace, joy & compassion in my life.

As I become A Compassionate Watcher, I am feeling my body as a source of experience, more stable & constant then my mind. I am using my body as an anchor for my awareness of the present moment, by helping my mind & body to grow calmer and more focused, to help me maintain my mindfulness throughout the day.

As My Compassionate Watcher, I am training myself to vividly experience external sensory objects, as I try to completely be the eye with form, the nose with smell, the ear with sound, the tongue with taste, and the body with touch.

And as My Compassionate Watcher, I am enjoying the experience of remaining in a state of perceptual awareness of all external sensory objects without decision.

I am also practicing visualizing myself as A Compassionate Watcher of all the spiritual love in the universe.

Start of visualization:

My Compassionate Watcher, you are the primordial energy of unconditional love who is manifesting inside my mind & body.

You have been given to me by God to be my conscience and you are helping me to maintain my connection to God, who is the source of all spiritual love, knowledge & energy in the universe. You are guiding me to connect with my universal source so you can help me to share in this continuous loving energy and so you can help me to live my life with great passion. To accomplish this I am using meditation to touch the present moment to become mindful of everything that is happening to me in the present moment, while it is happening, no matter what is.

As I connect with you, My Compassionate Watcher, I am touching universal understanding and I am seeing more deeply as this knowledge heals the wounds in my mind, as you help provide me with continuous love, joy, compassion, patience, kindness, goodness, faithfulness, humility, understanding, sensitivity & self-control.

As I meditate with all my heart, you are awakening in me as I continue to meditate and as I feel your power swelling in me. I do not need to do anything else since you are always with me. Everything is fine as I rest with you in the arms of God. With your help, I am seeing things clearly, understanding deeply and loving passionately.

As I enter deeply into the Present Moment, I am seeing the true nature of reality and this insight is liberating me from suffering and confusion. I love you, My Compassionate Watcher and I know you love me fully without reservations or conditions of any kind. You are here to help me & support me. I can only thank you for this by becoming the loving human being you are motivating me to be, as I endeavor to share unconditional love & nurture true friendship with everyone in my life, during my limited lifetime on Our Precious Mother Earth.

End of my visualization

**The Role of A Compassionate Watcher**

I become A Compassionate Watcher as I detach from & then start controlling all the life-enhancing mental activities in my conscious mind that will improve my life experiences, by using my thinking energy to prolong the life of my positive feelings of love, peace, joy & compassion and by thinking that life is being fair to me.

And

I become A Compassionate Watcher as I detach from & then start controlling all the negative life-diminishing mental activities in my conscious mind that will degrade my life experiences, by **not** using my thinking energy to prolong the life of my negative feelings of worry & stress or pain & suffering, by **not** thinking that life is being unfair to me.

Dr. Wayne Dyer describes in chapter five of his book, Your Sacred Self, how My Compassionate Watcher observes the activities of my mind, as the Witness who is doing the observing.

"Here from an invisible space outside of your physical body, the Witness is detached from your emotions, feelings and behaviors. Here the Witness lovingly watches your entire life transpire."

Dr. Dyer describes the Witness as,

"The Invisible I, that talks to the physical self. This is the thinker of the thoughts. This Compassionate Observer is not revealed with scientific instruments and doesn't appear on autopsy reports. When you are genuinely able to live in that spiritual domain of the Witness, then nothing goes wrong because wrong is not possible for the Witness."

"Within all of us is the eternal changeless dimension of our higher spiritual selves" [101]

I become A Compassionate Watcher as I observe all the revealed mental activities inside my mind.

To become A Compassionate Watcher, I take a mental step back from being inside my feelings, thoughts & mental images to begin to observe them from the outside. I ask My Compassionate Watcher to detach me from living **inside** of all my pleasant, neutral or painful feelings to become able to fully observe all the nuances of their behavior from **outside** of them, as I look back at them from the outside, as they try to influence me to think & act to satisfy their desires.

I make the commitment to My Compassionate Watcher to not follow the desires of my negative life-diminishing feelings, thoughts or mental images, when they motivate me to go back inside them & become one with them, but instead, I become fully detached from them and I simply observe them from outside, to become able to fully understand them, before I decide to kill them by not feeding them any new thinking energy to stop keeping them alive inside my mind.

And before I make a decision to indulge in any of the life-enhancing desires that are living inside my mind, as they motivate me to become one with them by following their directions when I allow them to take control my mind & actions, I ask My Compassionate Watcher to continue to observe them from the outside, so I do not become lost inside these pleasurable feelings, thoughts & images that will distract me from working on My Goals for Today.

My Compassionate Watcher practices Meditation to enable me to maintain a continuous connection to my internal source of unconditional love to provide me with powerful motivation to achieve continuous mindfulness of all my feelings, thoughts & images and to become able to eliminate all the negative unfair painful feelings in my conscious mind, as my internal source of unconditional love starts to feed my conscious mind with powerful feelings of **continuous** love, peace, joy & compassion.

# Chapter 10

## Practicing Meditation & Mindfulness

As I start applying The Wisdom of Children to my adult life each morning, I begin to practice Meditation & Mindfulness as soon as I wake up from sleep to the start of a new day.

Meditation is practicing Mindfulness to maintain my connection to the continuous present moment, which enables me to feel the continuous love, peace, joy & compassion that is flowing inside me, as this unconditional love flows through me from all the life in the universe.

And Meditation is practicing detachment from all the thoughts feelings & images in my conscious mind that are preventing me from achieving a state of Mindfulness.

A State of Mindfulness occurs when I begin to know what is happening inside my conscious mind in the present moment, while it is happening, no matter what it is. (Modified quote from What is Meditation by Rob Nairn)

As I achieve a state of Mindfulness, I become able to perceive all the thoughts, feelings & images in my conscious mind, clearly & correctly, without distortion or falsehood, as I become able to choose to live in the present moment without accepting distractions from the past or the future.

Achieving a state of mindfulness is made possible by following The Middle Path (or The Middle Way) of Meditation that Buddhists practice when they meditate. As Buddhists practice meditation, they simply observe, without additional mental effort and without striving for meditation results, as they observe all the mental activities inside their conscious minds without trying to control them and without trying to change them, as they concentrate on their breathing which helps to calm the conscious mind by reducing the energy & speed of the conscious mind's mental activities, similar to taking one's foot off the gas pedal when driving a car.

In this way, the meditator stops giving thinking energy (similar to cutting off the gas supply to the car's engine) to the feelings, thoughts & images in the meditator's conscious mind by not thinking about them so they run out of the thinking energy that they need to continue living inside the meditator's conscious mind. When they run out of this energy for living, they have no choice but to leave the conscious mind which results in the conscious mind's activities slowing down, as the conscious mind starts to calm, as the number of feelings, thoughts & images in the conscious mind is reduced.

When I follow The Middle Path of Meditation, I realize that I am not my feelings, thoughts & images because I can kill them by not feeding them the thinking energy that they need to stay alive inside my conscious mind, as I become a watcher of the activities in my conscious mind and as I become mindful of them, as I begin to know what is happening inside my conscious mind in the present moment, while it is happening, no matter what it is.

Unfortunately, I sometimes find meditating extremely difficult to practice, when the pain inside my conscious mind becomes intense, whenever I start to relive a powerful unfair memory that starts to generate new pain inside my conscious mind, as my desire to run away and hide from this intense pain becomes overwhelming, as this pain tries to take control of my conscious mind away from me.

Fortunately, I was born with an equally powerful stubborn streak which makes it difficult for me to give up and run away from pain, when I decide to continue meditating until the pain runs out of energy and disappears from my conscious mind. So, I just wait and feel the full intensity of the pain as I continue to observe it, as I strengthen my resolve to continue waiting for the pain to go away, by telling myself that the pain will eventually end. This painful waiting practice is part of the price that I am willing to pay to become able to gain the benefits that Practicing The Wisdom of Children will bring into my adult life. These benefits far outweigh any pain that I am required to endure. They are my reward for continuing the meditation practice, as they enable me to increase the love & friendship that I share with everyone in my life.

In this way, I become A Compassionate Watcher as I observe my mental activities, as I learn to understand them and then as I sympathize with their desire to take control of my conscious mind, as I remain in control of my conscious mind, by taking control of the thinking energy in my conscious mind to become able to choose the feelings, thoughts & images that I want to experience at this present time.

Once my conscious mind calms and enters a state of mindfulness & bliss, I start to give new thinking energy to the feelings, thoughts & images that I want to experience, as I watch the unwanted feelings, thoughts & images disappear from my conscious mind because I am no longer giving them the thinking energy that they need to feed on, to be able to stay alive inside my conscious mind. As these unwanted feelings, thoughts & images run out of the thinking energy for living that I am no longer supplying them, they start to disappear from my conscious mind, as my conscious mind becomes calm and becomes focused on the mental activities that I want to experience inside my conscious mind.

**How I Practice Meditation Each New Day of My Life**

1) As I wake up from sleep in the morning and I start Practicing The Wisdom of Children, I begin to observe all the mental activities in my conscious mind as I become A Compassionate Watcher who is the embodiment of my unconditional love as I start to become aware of the present moment, as I begin to practice Meditation which stops me from living inside the past, the future, my feelings, my thoughts, my imagination, or my dreams. Then, as I achieve Mindfulness I begin knowing what is happening inside my conscious mind in the present moment, while it is happening, no matter what it is. This practice enables me to reconnect to My Internal Source of Unconditional Love which connects me to the continuous love emanating from all the life in the universe, after a night of sleep & dreams.

Next, I begin to practice Choosing My Feelings by detaching from all the feelings in my conscious mind that are trying to control my conscious mind, as I become able to determine which feelings are harmful or beneficial to my future well-being before I choose to indulge in feeding new thinking energy to a feeling to increase its energy & prolong its life, as it lives inside my conscious mind. I am choosing to increase the energy of a feeling, only if, it will help motivate me to work on My Goals for Today.[6]

2) As I continue to practice Meditation & Mindfulness during the day, I am experiencing the benefits of choosing to increase the love, peace, joy & compassion that I am feeling, as I feel these benefits intermittently at first when I wake up in the morning and then for longer periods of time during the day, as my Meditation & Mindfulness allows me to continuously Choose My Feelings, as my connection to my internal source of unconditional love for all life becomes continuous, as my internal source of love supplies me with powerful love, peace, joy & compassion and with powerful motivation to accomplish My Goals for Today.

3) Then, when I take a relaxing break from my work during the day, I embrace the benefits of applying The Wisdom of Children to my life by realizing that, I am practicing Meditation continuously in the present moment of today, to manage my Mindfulness, to be able to say, "no" to blindly following the desires of my pleasant or painful feelings, to become able to detach from all my feelings by not feeding them any new thinking energy that will keep them alive, until I am able to determine which ones are harmful and which ones are beneficial to my future well-being, and only then am I deciding, whether or not to say, "Yes" to feeding thinking energy to a beneficial feeling, to indulge in it & keep it alive & active inside my conscious mind.

In this way, I enable my Meditation & Mindfulness to help me to practice Choosing My Feelings, as I work on My Goals for Today, as I increase the amount of unconditional love that I am generating, as I spiritually connect with all human beings in the world who have become my spiritual brothers & sisters, and as I start to share increasing love, peace, joy & compassion with all human beings that I meet today, especially with my friends & family.

Controlling my thinking energy so I can choose my feelings during the day is expressed concisely by My Son Wil, when he says,

"It is important for me to remember that I am not my feelings. I am not my mind either. I am the compassionate watcher that exists before thought. I am who I truly am when I'm not thinking. This primacy means that I have control over what I think about and how I feel. Life is entirely experiential. It flows through the filter of perception. Nothing exists for me divorced from how I perceive it. Thus, I can control my existence, make it pure, by controlling how I think so I can choose how I feel. This is free will."

(Quote from My Son Wil's Killing the Unfairness in My Memories section in Chapter 26 of Our Book One)

My Meditation practice is based on four separate meditation techniques:

**Control Meditation**

Control Meditation is practicing Mindfulness by mentally concentrating on the awareness of my breathing and by detaching from all the feelings, thoughts & images in my conscious mind, until my thinking slows down and my conscious mind becomes calm & tranquil.

**Release Meditation**

Release Meditation is practicing Mindfulness by releasing my mental concentration on my breathing so I can expand my mental awareness to include all the revealed activities of my conscious mind including all the feelings, thoughts & images in my conscious mind

**Mind & Body Meditation**

Mind & Body Meditation is practicing Mindfulness to connect me to the vast energy field of unconditional love emanating from all the life in the universe, as I absorb this love energy into my motivation batteries, as I start to feel my sense of belonging to all this life, as I start to feel totally loved by this universal life, and as all life becomes me & I become all life.

**Compassion Meditation**

Compassion Meditation is practicing Mindfulness to become able to fully reconnect to my compassion for all the life that surrounds me, as my compassion expands out into the world to help increase the amount of unconditional love & forgiveness being shared by all human beings on Our Precious Mother Earth.

We will now discuss each of these meditation techniques in detail.

# Chapter 11

## Control Meditation

Control Meditation is practicing mindfulness by mentally concentrating on the awareness of my breathing and by detaching from all the feelings, thoughts & images in my conscious mind, until my thinking slows down and my conscious mind becomes calm & tranquil.

I am practicing Control Meditation to take my concentration away from my existing mental distractions that may be trying to stop me from working on my goals. Concentrating on my breathing reduces my compulsive thinking about my existing distractions, as it slows down my mental activity, which allows my mind & body to calm down, which allows My Compassionate Watcher to regain full control on all of my conscious mind's thinking energy by detaching from the existing distractions in my conscious mind, to enable me to use the full power of my thinking energy to work on my goals.

Control Meditation feeds my uncontrolled thinking energy to the awareness of my breathing, to reduce the available uncontrolled thinking energy that is feeding my existing distractions, such as the uncontrolled random feelings, thoughts & images of my daydreaming or the uncontrolled compulsively thinking about the worry & stress in my life or the uncontrolled desires of My Ego, as I ask My Compassionate Watcher to stop my uncontrolled thinking energy from feeding my existing distractions, as My Compassionate Watcher regains full control of all of my conscious mind's thinking energy, as it starts to feed the full power of my thinking energy to accomplishing my goals.

As I concentrate, on my awareness of breathing in & out, I am counting my breaths from 1 to 21, and I am repeating the counting process, starting over again at 1, until my distractions have disappeared from my conscious mind. Becoming aware of my breathing creates space between my uncontrolled thoughts which gives My Compassionate Watcher a window to look inside my conscious mind to become able to understand what is causing my distractions and to become able to stop them from distracting me.

Now that I have control over my distractions, I am able to manage my conscious mind & actions. I may still be thinking but I am controlling what I think about as I practice meditation & mindfulness to know, what is happening in my conscious mind in the present moment, while it is happening, no matter what it is. [92]

**Questions about My Control Meditation Q-166:**

1) How do I silently experience the gap between breathing in & breathing out to allow me to experience the eternal in the present moment? [93]

2) How does counting from 1 to 21 help me to calm my mind? [94]

3) When I am mentally distracted by weak low-energy random feelings, thoughts & images, how do I gently stop my distractions by concentrating on my breathing?

4) How do I stop my compulsive thinking, worrying & stressing out, to help me calm my mind so I can begin to rest in love, peace, joy & compassion?

5) How do I calm my mind so I can fully concentrate on accomplishing My Goals for Today? [95]

The next step in increasing my meditation power to become able to manage my mind & actions, is to let go of concentrating on my breathing. When this level of meditation begins there is no sense of my meditation happening. There is just the relaxed experience of feelings, thoughts & images without any sense of My Compassionate Watcher experiencing them. I have released my concentration on my breathing to allow My Compassionate Watcher to observe all the activities of my conscious mind, so I can spot a new powerful feeling, thought or image, when it tries to take control of my mind & my future actions.

# Chapter 12

## Release Meditation

Release Meditation is practicing mindfulness by releasing my mental concentration on my breathing so I can expand my mental awareness to include all the revealed activities of my conscious mind including all the feelings, thoughts & images in my conscious mind

And Release Meditation expands the awareness of my conscious mind to become able to spot any new distractions as they enter my conscious mind, as they try to take control of my conscious mind & actions by convincing me to grasp onto the desire for action embedded in a new feeling, thought or image which may be trying to stop me from working on My Goals.

When I spot a new distraction, I am using the power of My Compassionate Watcher & the powerful motivation of my internal source of unconditional love to detach from the new distraction and then eliminate it from my conscious mind when it tries to stop me from working on my goals

### Becoming a Master of Release Meditation

I am becoming A Master of Release Meditation as I use meditation to Rest in the Arms of God & Just Be without becoming attached to any feelings, thoughts & images that my awareness of my connection to all the life surrounding me is offering me.

This produces the experience of the absolute, spontaneous, non-dual awareness of my primordial state. In this state of being, I do not have to make any effort. There is nothing further to be accomplished. I only have to remain detached & un-distracted, so that I do not jump on any uncontrollable horses that may try to carry me away from the goals that I am working on, as these wild horses become distracting feelings thoughts, & images in my conscious mind when I allow them to start controlling my mind & future actions.

I am practicing Release Meditation during the present moment of each new day of my life to enable My Compassionate Watcher to manage my mind & actions, to become able to prevent any new distracting desires contained inside my feelings, thoughts or images from stopping me from working on The Goals for My life, goals that are designed to fulfill the unique purpose and to experience the special meaning of my life.

## Using Control & Release Meditation as Team Players

The Key to being able to live continuously in the Present Moment is using Control & Release Meditation as Team Players to achieve mindfulness to enable me to maintain my awareness of all the activities of my conscious mind & body during the day.

This continuous awareness of my mind & body is anchoring me to the present moment and enabling me to enjoy all the physical & mental activities in my life, without losing control of my conscious mind to minor distractions or powerful feelings that may want to take control away from My Compassionate Watcher, or may want to disconnect me from my internal source of unconditional love, so they can start to take control of my life as they encourage me to follow the dictates of my negative life-diminishing feelings, my compulsive thinking or My Ego.

The continuous awareness of my mind & body are helping me to embrace the present moment so I can live my life with great passion as I become aware of all the activities in my mind & body and as I become aware of everything that is happening around me in the external world while it is happening in the present moment.

How do I enable Control & Release Meditation to work together to achieve Mindfulness? Q-167

# Chapter 13

## Mind & Body Meditation

Mind & Body Meditation is practicing Mindfulness to connect me to the vast energy field of unconditional love emanating from all the life in the universe, as I absorb this love energy into my motivation batteries, as I start to feel my sense of belonging to all this life, as I start to feel totally loved by this universal life, and as all life becomes me & I become all life.

After I complete my control & release meditation practices, I am practicing mind & body meditation. I am closing my eyes and feeling the stillness of My Compassionate Watcher. Then, I am imagining My Compassionate Watcher living inside my mind & body as a field of pure potential & unlimited unconditional love that is part of the pure eternal spiritual energy field of the universe. This is the love energy that makes me who I am. I am focusing exclusively on the energy field of the unconditional love from all the life in the universe as My Compassionate Watcher begins to merge with this energy field of unconditional love.

Then, as my conscious mind becomes filled with an all-encompassing experience of being joined to this vast universal energy field of unconditional love, I start to leave the feelings of my mind & body behind, while I sit in my meditation chair, as I start to feel an out of body experience, as my internal source of unconditional love merges into the vast energy field of all the life in the universe. Now, I feel totally accepted & loved by all this life, as I begin resting in this field of pure contentment for as long as I need to be, as I absorb this energy of life into my motivation batteries that live inside me, as I Rest in the Arms of God & Just Be, as I feel the joy that I am sharing with all this life, as I feel my sense of belonging to all this life, as my internal source of unconditional love connects me with God who is the source of all the unconditional love in the universe. Now, all life is inside me and I am inside all life.[97]

Then, I am becoming mentally aware, once again, of my physical body, my breathing, and my physical senses, as I sit in my meditation chair. I am opening my eyes and looking at my surroundings without labeling them mentally and I am continuing to feel the unconditional love from my internal source of unconditional love, as I start to work on my goals for the day. Having access to the energy field of all the life in the universe is truly liberating. This state is called My Awareness of My Connection to All Life that I experience as Resting in the Arms of God & Just Being. This is an experience of profound tranquility, love, peace, joy, compassion & intense aliveness.

By practicing mind & body meditation, I am awakening out of my dream of identification with the negativity of my dream world, which is contained in my random thoughts or my compulsive thinking about the worry & stress in my life, which occurs, when my conscious mind absorbs my uncontrolled thinking energy and transforms it into the compulsive thoughts inside my dream world that I create in my conscious mind when I cannot stop my compulsive thinking.

My Compassionate Watcher is helping me to withdraw from my dream world of random thoughts, compulsive thinking & the desires of My Ego, by practicing control & release meditation to achieve mindfulness, to think less and to connect to the unconditional love that is being generated by my internal source of unconditional love, which is living inside my mind & body.

My mind & body meditation practice is allowing me to stop my compulsive thinking, by enabling me to release all my uncontrolled thinking energy that was being used to power my worry & stress, so I can now use this liberated energy to fully reconnect to my awareness of my internal source of unconditional love that is helping to keep me aware of the present moment, and that is helping to anchor me in the Now, by connecting me to the awareness of my mind & body, as I experience its connection to all the life in the universe. [98]

I am becoming conscious of the unconditional love that is flowing into my conscious mind from my internal source of unconditional love, by taking my mental attention away from my thinking, and instead, I am directing my mental attention into my mind & body where my internal source of unconditional love lives. I am feeling the unconditional love as the energy field that is giving spiritual power to my mind & body.

I am practicing mind & body meditation to feel this energy of love more fully, and to allow this energy field of love to help motivate me to pursue my goals for the day, by enabling me to feel intense joy emanating from my awareness of my connection to the primordial energy of unconditional love that I am sharing with all the life in the universe.[99]

How do I practice Mind & Body Meditation to connect me to the spiritual energy of the unconditional love that is living inside all the life in the universe, to become able to recharge my motivational batteries and to generate increasing love, peace, joy & compassion in my life? Q-168

# Chapter 14

## Compassion Meditation

Compassion Meditation is practicing mindfulness to become able to fully reconnect to my compassion for all the life that surrounds me, as my compassion expands out into the world to help increase the amount of unconditional love & forgiveness being shared by all human beings on Our Precious Mother Earth.

As I experience compassion, I start to feel a burning desire to help all the children in our world to learn The Wisdom of Children, to enable them to kill all the unresolved pain in their conscious minds by practicing forgiveness, to stop this suffering from hurting them in the future.

To help all the children in the world, I am asking the readers of our books to teach each child in their family, **the wisdom of how a child's young mind should work** to successfully kill all the unresolved pain & suffering in a child's life, as the parents & guardians of young children work with each child individually to help make this killing process a success. (We will discuss how to help the children in our lives in greater detail in Our Book Four)

When the child becomes able to kill this unresolved pain & suffering, the child's mind will automatically start to fully reconnect with the internal source of unconditional love that the child was born possessing, a powerful continuous love that fuels the child's desire to love everyone & everything in the child's life with great passion.

Of course, the parents & guardians must first learn how to do this inside their adult minds before they can start teaching the children in their lives, by practicing The Nine Steps to Emotional Freedom in Chapter 13 of Our Book One or by using their own personal wisdom that they acquired as they grew up.

To love all the Children in the World
Is to become
A child again

As I help the children I know to continue
Loving everyone & everything in their lives
With great passion

This is my dream
And with the help of the child living inside me
It is becoming my reality

I am Loving All The Children in the world by writing the Practicing The Wisdom of Children series of books with the help of my son, to provide a legacy of wisdom from our ancestors that will inspire parents & guardians to teach this wisdom to the their children, starting with the child that is living inside each adult reader of our books.

As I write, my compassion keeps reminding me that I do not want any child to go through the suffering that I went through in my life when I became disconnected from my internal source of continuous love, peace, joy & compassion for long periods of time during my childhood, when I did not know how to stop my unresolved pain & suffering from hurting me.

How is my compassion motivating me to help someone in my life today?

How successful have I been in the last 24 hours in practicing Compassion Meditation to help My Compassionate Watcher to connect me to the universal compassion living in the external world of people & events, a compassion that I am helping to share with all the life on Our Precious Mother Earth? Q-169

# Chapter 15

## Becoming A Master of Meditation

Meditation techniques are easy to learn and difficult to implement into my life.

During the day when I am working on my goals, my negative habit energies, such as my habitual desire to procrastinate or my daydreaming, may allow the desires of My Ego to take control of me, whenever I start to feel worry & stress or pain & anger in my life.

This suffering which I want to avoid in the future helps to motivate me to become a Master of Meditation & Mindfulness to enable me to maintain continuous control of my mind & actions in the future, so I can kill all the unresolved pain & suffering that may try to live inside my conscious mind.

Pema Chodron, a Buddhist Nun & bestselling author recommends that we practice for a minimum of ten years to master meditation & mindfulness, to help us increase the power of unconditional love in all aspects of our lives. To accomplish this we need to learn how to kill all the major unresolved pain & suffering in our memories that is preventing us from fully reconnecting with our internal source of powerful unconditional love.[100]

Some gifted human beings can accomplish this in a few months, because they have a small amount of unresolved pain & suffering buried inside their unfair memories that they need to learn how to kill.

Unfortunately, it took me more than ten years to kill the large amount of unfair pain that was stored in My Room of Memories in my subconscious mind, pain that was generating unfair suffering into my conscious mind each new day of my life, as I grew up.

Please be patience with your progress as you start to become a
Master of Meditation & Mindfulness, as you begin to kill all the
major unresolved pain & suffering in your memories to increase the
amount unconditional love that you will become able to share with
those you love, in all aspects of your life.

How is my daily meditation practice helping me to implement
Mindfulness into all aspects of my life to help me to complete My
Goals for Today, as I maintain my connection to my internal source
of universal love, peace, joy & compassion that I am sharing with all
the life that surrounds me, especially with my friends & family?

# Chapter 16

## Increasing the Unconditional Love in My Life

I am learning the wisdom of how my mind should work, so I can ask my mind to help me experience increasing unconditional love each new day of my life, to increase my ability to share this healthy self-love with all the life that surrounds me, especially with my friends & family.

To experience increasing love, peace, joy & compassion, I am learning to choose what I experience each new day of my life which requires that I gain and maintain control of my mind & actions, by learning how to mediate to achieve mindfulness.

Mindfulness is asking My Compassionate Watcher to help me know what is happening inside my mind in the present moment, while it is happening, no matter what it is. [102]

My Daily Goal is to live in mindfulness for twenty-four hours each day so I can maintain a continuous connection to My Internal Source of Unconditional Love for all life.

To be truly here in the Now in the Present Moment is my objective, my ultimate task, my ultimate quest & my ultimate achievement, which occurs whenever I am able to kill the unresolved pain & suffering in my conscious mind that is blocking my pathway to my internal source of unconditional love, an internal source of love that I was born possessing, as I fully reconnect to this powerful source of love which helps me to share unconditional love & nurture true friendship with those I love during the continuous present moment of each new day of my life. [103]

Enjoying the present moment occurs when I practice meditation to achieve mindfulness and when I use the wisdom of The Science of My Mind that I have proven to be true, to help me to manage my mind & actions to enable me to maintain my connection to my internal source of unconditional love for all life.

I am beginning to realize that my conscious mind rests in a state of purity & wholeness, when I am fully connected to my external source of unconditional love from all the life that is surrounding me, which provides my internal source of unconditional love with the power that it needs to cleanse my conscious mind of all the negative life-diminishing feelings, thoughts & images that may bring impurity into my mind. And since I believe that My Creator who I call God is the source of all the unconditional love in the universe, I can restate this understanding by saying:

I become A Compassionate Watcher when I Rest Quietly in the Arms of God, as I feel my connection to my internal source of love, peace, joy & compassion & my connection to all the love in the universe, as My Compassionate Watcher controls the mental activities of my conscious mind that are improving my life experiences, as I increase the power of my positive life-enhancing feelings, thoughts & images by feeding them my thinking energy to enhance & prolong their life.[104]

When I become A Compassionate Watcher, unconditional love automatically starts to flow continuously through my mind & body from my internal connection to God, when I practice meditation to help me to use the power & energy of mindfulness to cleanse my conscious mind of all my negative feelings, thoughts & images. This continuous stream of love, peace, joy & compassion flows from my internal source of unconditional love into my conscious mind and gives me a sense of belonging to all life in the universe which is the highest form of human social experience according to Dr. Abraham Maslow.

In contrast, whenever I become My Ego and it starts to control me, I start to feel separate from all the life that surrounds me, as My Ego starts to convince me to treat others as adversaries in a battle to get a share of the scare resources in the external world, such as external joy & money that are available to me, only if, I do what My Ego desires.[105]

(Please refer to Practicing The Wisdom of Children is Hazardous to My Ego! Section in Chapter 18 of Our Book One)

How do I ask My Compassionate Watcher to help me increase the unconditional love in my life? Q-171

# Chapter 17

## Managing My Feelings to Achieve Total Realization

To achieve Total Realization, I am becoming free of the unresolved pain & suffering in my conscious mind, by practicing The Nine Steps to Emotional Freedom which enables me to fully reconnect to my internal source of unconditional love for all the life in the universe that I was born possessing, a love that supplies me with powerful passion for living my life to the full.

And I am using meditation practice to achieve continuous mindfulness to manage all my feelings, so I can experience **continuous** love, peace, joy & compassion during my day, as I achieve Total Realization which allows me to Rest in the Arms of God & Just Be.[107]

When I reach the mental state of Total Realization, I no longer cause pain & suffering in my life and instead I experience enlightenment. I become enlightened when all my inherent enlightened qualities of love, peace, joy, compassion, understanding, equality & clarity of the truth & untruth in my conscious mind are continuously experienced by me, which becomes the mental state of achieving the total mental realization of what is happening inside my conscious mind and what is happening around me in the external world of people & events, in the present moment, which prevents all my previous delusions & my self-inflicted pain & suffering from re-occurring inside my conscious mind.

With my powerful energy of unconditional love and my mastery of the techniques of using meditation & mindfulness to achieve total realization of what is happening in the present moment, I am sharing increasing unconditional love with my family & friends to help them to fully reconnect with their source of unconditional love that is living inside each of them, so they can experience increasing love, peace, joy & compassion in their lives as this energy of unconditional love connects them to all the life in the universe and connects them to all human beings on Our Precious Mother Earth, as they become members of one universal spiritual family who share unconditional love & nurture true friendship with each other.

The more I am watching my feelings, thoughts & images each moment of the day, the more control I have over my motivation, as I manage the amount of thinking energy that I am feeding my sprouted memory seeds, My Ego or the new events in my life, with no thinking energy for my negative feelings and powerful thinking energy for my positive feelings.

When My Compassionate Watcher observes a negative feeling and does not think about it, it starves the feeling of thinking energy, so it runs out of energy & dies and when My Compassionate Watcher thinks about a positive feeling, it may decide to feed the feeling new thinking energy to help this feeling become more powerful & live longer inside me.

This observation and control process is called Mindfulness, which enables My Compassionate Watcher, to know, what is happening inside my mind in the present moment, while it is happening, no matter what it is. [106]

In Summary:

I am asking My Compassionate Watcher to help me use meditation & mindfulness to achieve Total Realization, to help me manage my mind & actions so I can experience increasing love, peace, joy & compassion during each new day of my life and less suffering each day, as I learn to manage my feelings, as I accomplish my goals for the day, and I travel the path of Total Realization.

How do I use Meditation practice to achieve Mindfulness to manage all my feelings, so I can experience Total Realization? Q-172

# Chapter 18

## How My Mind Should Work

During my daily Meditation & Mindfulness practice, I am using the knowledge of how my mind actually works and my understanding of The Nine Steps to Emotional Freedom from Our Book One, to kill any Unresolved Pain & Suffering that may enter my conscious mind today. Then, I become able to understand how my mind should work in the future to keep my conscious mind free of any new pain & suffering that may try to enter my life.

Then, I will no longer have the desire to run away from any new unfair pain that may enter my future life, when I start reliving a painful memory because I have learned how to kill the major source of unresolved pain & suffering in my unfair memories and I will no longer suppress any new negative feelings from the external world of people & events that may enter my conscious mind because I now know how to stop the pain & suffering from hurting me.

The thinking energy that I used to kill this pain & suffering is now being liberated for new work, so I can now add it to the energy reserves inside my conscious mind, energy reserves that I use each day to increase the life-enhancing motivation that I need to power my passion for living. My capacity to feel joy is invigorated and refreshed. especially when I kill off any remaining unresolved pain & suffering that is still hidden inside my unfair memories, so that someday after I have killed the energy reserves of all the painful memories that I have been reliving, I will wake up each new morning of my life and only feel positive life-enhancing feelings from my memories, whenever I start to relive a now painless memory during the day.

I encourage you to look inside your mind to understand how your mind works by answering the questions for truth so you can understand the truth & the untruth contained in the feelings, thoughts & images that are living inside your conscious mind, as you begin your quest to understand how your mind should work to keep it free of untruth in the future.

Then, please practice The Nine Steps To Emotional Freedom from Our Book One to fully reconnect with your Internal Childhood Source of Unconditional Love to enable you to use this love & forgiveness to kill any new unresolved pain & suffering in your life until it is gone forever, so you can start to feel continuous love, peace, joy & compassion in your daily life that you can share with your friends & family.

Does your mind work as we have described as Our Books One & Two? If not. Why Not?

How should my mind work to free itself of any new untruth or any new unresolved pain & suffering, so I can experience **continuous** love, peace, joy & compassion today? Q-173

**Please Forgive Us**

The wisdom in Our Book Two is very repetitive. We have written it this way on purpose to help you loosen the grip that your ego may have on you. Please forgive me & my son for this repetition.

"Aristotle once commented on the importance of repetition in education by noting, "It is frequent repetition that produces a natural tendency." Many teachers strive to help their students acquire new skills by using repetition as a highly effective way to do so, for as Aristotle mentions, it is how tasks and knowledge can become second nature for students.

Repetition is a key learning aid because it helps transition a skill from the conscious to the subconscious. Through repetition, a skill is practiced and rehearsed over time and gradually becomes easier. As the student improves, he does not need to think consciously about the skill, which has become automatic, such as mastering the skill of riding a bicycle.

This is how repetition makes the skill of Practicing The Wisdom of Children easier to learn & perfect." (Modified quote from Focus & Repetition in Learning)

The next chapter will reduce all this repetition into concise questions, whose answers will enable you to more easily understand and then practice The Wisdom of Children in your life.

# Chapter 19

## Practicing Wisdom Each Day

**A) I am practicing The Nine Steps to Emotional Freedom from unresolved pain & suffering by:**

Step 1 - Practicing Detachment to stop my distractions from trying to control me.

Step 2 - Practicing Friendship with my feelings, thoughts & images to understand why they are living inside my mind.

Step 3 - Controlling My Mind to accomplish my goals for today.

Step 4 - Practicing Fairness to enable my future life to be fair to me.

Step 5 - Practicing Forgiveness to unblock the pathway to my internal source of love, peace, joy & compassion

Step 6 - Choosing My Feelings that I want to experience & killing my feelings that try to hurt me.

Step 7 - Practicing Self-Discipline to share unconditional love & forgiveness with everyone in my life.

Step 8 - Practicing Thankfulness to nurture true friendship with everyone in my life.

Step 9 - Sharing All The Love in The Universe to recharge my internal source of unconditional love.

As I practice each of the nine steps, I see nothing in my friends & family but their childhood ability to love me, as I continue to love them and I prepare to forgive them for any unfair pain & suffering they may create in my life.

And I am answering these questions:

Am I working on my goals for today, instead of waiting for feelings to motivate me to act, as I embrace the motivation contained in the unconditional love that is living inside me, to work on my goals, even though I may start reliving a demotivating primordial fear of future loss or failure?

Can I remember when I felt immense love for all the life around me, when I was a young child, as I shared new fun & adventures with my family & friends? Q-1

Am I embracing my childhood memory of this powerful love as my proof that I may be able to fully reconnect with my childhood ability to love my life with great passion?

And will I pay any price that is required to fully reconnect to the passion of my childhood, to enable me to feel continuous love, peace, joy & compassion in my adult life? Why? Q-5

(Please refer to Chapter 13 of Our Book One to increase your understanding of the nine steps to emotional freedom from unresolved pain & suffering)

## B) Then, I am practicing Byron Katie's Wisdom by:

Answering the question, "What is creating this?" about every mental activity in my conscious mind to become able to judge what is real.[83] about the original decisions I make in my life.

An Original Decision is defined as the forming of an evaluation, opinion, estimate, notion or conclusion about the truth of the events in my life that I add to The Story of My Life that I create in my mind each day. These events live inside my conscious mind as my feelings, thoughts & images of the external world, my dreams, my memories & my thinking.[78] To understand them, I am asking The Questions For Truth:

1) Are the feelings, thoughts & images in my mind a true description of my past, present or future life?

2) How do I test my feelings, thoughts & images for truth?

3) What impact will a revised decision about the truth or untruth of a feeling, thought or image have on my life?

4) How do I ask for forgiveness when I hurt someone or I hurt my life by making an untrue Original Decision?

(Please refer to the Obtaining Help from Byron Katie section in Chapter 1 of Our Book Two to increase your understanding of the wisdom of Byron Katie)

# Chapter 20

## Questions to Answer in My Own Words

"We have provided you with a list of questions from Our Book Two that will help you to master The Wisdom of Children. Hopefully, you have already answered some of the questions in your own words as you read through Our Book Two. Please write down your answers to the questions you have not answered and then store all your answers in a secure location that you can access in the future, as you use these answers to help you to become a master of The Wisdom of Children." (Modified Quote from the Questions to Answer in My Own Words section in Chapter 31 of Our Book One)

**Introduction**

Can I remember when I felt immense love for all the life around me, when I was a young child, as I shared new fun & adventures with my family & friends? Q-1

Will I pay any price that is required to fully reconnect to the passion of my childhood, to enable me to feel continuous love, peace, joy & compassion in my adult life? Why? Q-5

Is it possible to believe that The Wisdom of Children may help me to increase the joy & happiness in my adult life? Why? Q-11

Why do I lose my internal connection to unconditional love when I run away from the pain & suffering that my memories generate inside my conscious mind? Why do I allow this to occur and how can I prevent it in the future? Q-138

How will I share love with each person that I meet today? Q-152

How will I practice the Nine Steps to Emotional Freedom to enable me to kill any new feelings of pain & suffering that may enter my life today? Q-153

How will I practice controlling my thinking energy so I can stay fully connected to my internal source of love today, to enable me to greet those I meet today with abundant feelings of love that they will feel when they look into my eyes? Q-154

## Chapter 1 - My Image of the World that I Create in My Mind

Based on my understanding of how my mind works, how do I recreate the external world inside my mind? Q-155

Am I afraid to look inside My Mind at my painful memories? Why? Q-156

Why do I regard my sprouted memory seeds as if they were dreams until I can find out if they are true or untrue? Q-157

What are the benefits for my future joy & happiness when I answer The Questions for Truth? Q-158

How do I practice managing my sprouted memory seeds, to become able to increase the love, peace, joy & compassion in my life that I can share with my friends & family? Q-159
Q-159

## Chapter 3 - Learning to Manage My Worrying Process

How do I reduce the amount of worrying about my fear of future failure or loss that my memories, My Ego, or new events in my life may create inside my conscious mind? Q-160

## Chapter 6 - The Evolution of Family & Social Nurturing Skills

How can we help men to improve their qualities of emotional openness, compassion, tenderness & sensitivity, in family & social relationships? Q-161

How do I nurture the sharing of love & joy in my relationships, without also generating unintentional pain & suffering? Q-162

## Chapter 7 - My Separated Nature

How do I become a separated person? Q-163

## Chapter 8 - The Golden Rule of Conduct

What is The Golden Rule of Conduct? Q-164

How do I live by The Golden Rule of Conduct? Q-165

## Chapter 11 - Control Meditation

Questions about My Control Meditation Q-166

1) How do I silently experience the gap between breathing in & breathing out to allow me to experience the eternal in the present moment? [93]

2) How does counting from 1 to 21 help me to calm my mind? [94]

3) When I am mentally distracted by weak low-energy random feelings, thoughts & images, how do I gently stop my distractions by concentrating on my breathing?

4) How do I stop my compulsive thinking, worrying & stressing out, to help me calm my mind so I can begin to rest in love, peace, joy & compassion?

5) How do I calm my mind so I can fully concentrate on accomplishing My Goals for Today? [95]

## Chapter 12 - Release Meditation

How do I enable Control & Release Meditation to work together to achieve Mindfulness? Q-167

## Chapter 13 - Mind & Body Meditation

How do I practice Mind & Body Meditation to connect me to the spiritual energy of the unconditional love that is living inside all the life in the universe, to be able to recharge my motivational batteries and to generate increasing love, peace, joy & compassion in my life? Q-168

## Chapter 14 - Compassionate Meditation

How successful have I been in the last 24 hours in practicing Compassion Meditation to help My Compassionate Watcher to connect me to the universal compassion living in the external world of people & events, a compassion that I am helping to share with all the life on Our Precious Mother Earth? Q-169

## Chapter 15 - Becoming A Master of Meditation

How is my daily meditation practice helping me to implement Mindfulness into all aspects of my life to help me to complete My Goals for Today, as I maintain my connection to my internal source of universal love, peace, joy & compassion that I am sharing with all the life that surrounds me, especially my friends & family? Q-170

## Chapter 16 - The Role of My Compassionate Watcher

How do I ask My Compassionate Watcher to help me increase the unconditional love in my life? Q-171

## Chapter 17 - Managing My Feelings to Achieve Total Realization

How do I use Meditation practice to achieve Mindfulness to manage all my feelings, so I can experience Total Realization? Q-172

## Chapter 18 - Using the Wisdom of How My Mind Works

How should my mind work to free itself of any new untruth or any new unresolved pain & suffering, so I can experience **continuous** love, peace, joy & compassion today? Q-173

# Recommended Books & Videos

## The Nature of Unconditional Love

Loving What Is by Byron Katie – Highly Recommended!
The Absorbent Mind by Maria Montessori
The Montessori Method by Maria Montessori
The Secret Millionaire TV Series
Stick Up for Yourself! Every Kid's Guide to Personal Power &
Positive Self-Esteem by Gershen Kaufman
The Natural History of Love by Morton Hunt
Open Marriage by Nena & George O'Neill
The Five Love Languages by Gary Chapman

## Unconditional Love for All Life in the Universe

Earth The Power of the Planet presented by Iain Stewart - BBC
miniseries - Highly Recommended!
Evolution DVD by Nova - PBS Mini Series - Narrated by Liam
Neeson
Unlocking the Mystery of Life DVD by Illustra Media
The Elegant Universe DVD by Nova - PBS Mini Series
The Elegant Universe book by Brian Greene
Cosmic Voyage DVD by Imax

## Learning to Love Other Human Beings

Zen Heart by Ezra Bayda - Highly Recommended!
Toward a Psychology of Being, 3rd Edition by Abraham H. Maslow
The Seven Habits of Highly Effective People by Stephen Covey
The Eighth Habit by Stephen Covey
The Fountainhead novel by Ayn Rand

## Love for God

How to Know God - Book & DVD by Deepak Chopra - Highly
Recommended!

The Third Jesus by Deepak Chopra
Living Buddha Living Christ by Thich Nhat Hanh
Going Home, Jesus and Buddha as Brothers by Thich Nhat Hanh
How to Hear From God by Joyce Meyer
The Good Heart, A Buddhist Perspective on the Teachings of Jesus
by the 14th Dalai Lama

## Meditation & Mindfulness

Diamond Mind by Rob Nairn - Highly Recommended!
What is Meditation by Rob Nairn

## Living Spiritually

Many Lives, Many Masters" by psychotherapist Dr. Brian Weiss -
Highly Recommended!

## Habit Energies

Feel the Fear and Do It Anyway by Susan Jeffers - Highly
Recommended!
Understanding Our Mind by Thich Nhat Hanh
Buddha Mind, Buddha Body by Thich Nhat Hanh

## The Ego

Your Sacred Self by Wayne Dyer - Highly Recommended!
Understanding The Power of Now by Eckhart Tolle
The Power of Now by Eckhart Tolle
Stillness Speaks by Eckhart Tolle
A New Earth by Eckhart Tolle

## Procrastination

Procrastination, Why You Do It, What To Do About It by Jane
Burka & Lenora Yuen - Highly Recommended!

## Forgiveness of False Pride & Self Hate

Compassion and Self Hate by Theodore Isaac Rubin - Highly
Recommended!
Neurosis And Human Growth by Karen Horney

**Creating Personal Wealth & Personal Power**

The Seven Spiritual Laws of Success by Deepak Chopra - Book &
DVD  - Highly Recommended!
Wishes Fulfilled by Wayne Dyer

# Bibliography

The bibliography contains references to the literary & video material of the authors who have inspired us. My Son & I are indebted to these authors to whom we offer our thanks and our respect & admiration.

We apologize to any authors whose wisdom we may have used without referencing their literary material in Our Book Two. Please advise us so we can include the proper references in future revisions of Our Book Two.

The References also contain specialized definitions that we have created to help the reader to understand the wisdom in Our Book Two.

73 - Daring Steps Toward Fearlessness by Ringu Tulku - Pages 195 to 220

74 - Wild Awakening – The Heart of Mahamudra and Dzogchen by Dzogchen Ponlop – Page 84

75 - Question 20 from Dad's Summary of Condensed Meditation Practice

76 - Buddhism with an Attitude by B. Alan Wallace – Page 106

77 - Deepak Chopra suggests 60,000 to 80,000 thoughts per day

78- Specialized Definition by Bill Coulson

79 - Loving What Is by Byron Katie – Page 97

80 - Loving What Is by Byron Katie – Page 13

81 - Loving What Is by Byron Katie – Page 292

82 - Loving What Is by Byron Katie – Page 1

83 - Zen Heart by Ezra Bayda – Pages 22 & 96

84 -The Marriage Institution - http://balunywa.blogspot.com/

85 - Dictionary definition

86 - The Book of Secrets by Deepak Chopra - Page 212

87 - Your Sacred Self by Dr. Wayne Dyer - Page 26

88 - Adapted from "The Christopher Newsletter"

89 - Buddha Mind, Buddha Body by Thich Nhat Hanh – Page 2

90 - Buddha Mind, Buddha Body by Thich Nhat Hanh – Page 3
91 - Buddha Mind, Buddha Body by Thich Nhat Hanh – Page 22
92 - Diamond Mind by Rob Nairn - Page 24
93 - Wild Awakening – The Heart of Mahamudra and Dzogchen by
      Dzogchen Ponlop – Page 114
94 - Diamond Mind by Rob Nairn - Page 24
95 - Question 36 from Draft # 4 of Dad's Summary of Diamond
      Mind by Rob Nairn
96 - Causes of My Habit Energies by Bill Coulson - Section A –
      Question 35
97 - The Power of Now by Eckhart Tolle – Page 109
98 - Buddhism with an Attitude by B. Alan Wallace - Page 86
99 - Practicing The Power of Now by Eckhart Tolle - Pages 59 to 63
100 - Pure Meditation CD by Pema Chodron
101 - Your Sacred Self by Dr. Wayne Dyer - Pages 115-117
102 - Diamond Mind by Rob Nairn - Page 24
103 - Question 7 – Dad's Meditation for Seven Point Mind Training
104 - Question 8 – Dad's Meditation for Seven Point Mind Training
105 - Living Dreaming Dying by Bob Nairn – Pages 119 - 124
106 - Diamond Mind by Rob Nairn - Page 24
107 - Specialized Definition by Bill Coulson

# About the Author

William (Bill) Coulson experienced the reality of The Wisdom of Children in his everyday life as a young child, whenever he received unconditional love or forgiveness, especially when he did not deserve it, from a childhood friend, a family member or one of his teachers, who continued to offer him wonderful opportunities for fun & adventures during his childhood in a small rural farming community in Nova Scotia, Canada.

A quote from Bill, "When I became an adult, l began to understand how it is possible to relive the powerful unconditional love of my childhood by embracing the love from everyone around me, as I once did when I was a child, when I intuitively understood that the primary purpose of my life is to share unconditional love & nurture true friendship with my friends & family.

The wisdom I learned as I reconnected with my childhood ability to love life passionately enabled me to help other adults to kill the pain & suffering in their lives that was preventing them from feeling the continuous love, peace, joy & compassion of their childhood during each moment of every day of their future adult lives.

This is why I wrote our book called "Practicing The Wisdom of Children" with the help of my son, so I could leave a legacy of wisdom for my friends & family and my future grandchildren, so they will become able to protect their childhood ability to love life passionately and not lose it as I did and then have to find it again. And now this desire to help other human beings has expanded to include you, the reader of our book, who will benefit from practicing this wisdom, as you begin sharing the increasing unconditional love that this wisdom will bring into your future life.

When we are born, each of us is given a compelling desire to seek a unique & special purpose for our life that motivates us to start asking questions about the meaning of our lives on Earth, whose answers will help us to understand why each of us is given this opportunity to live a potentially wonderful human life, as we begin to ask & answer these questions:

> Who am I?
> Where did I come from?
> Why am I here on Earth?
> What is my life's purpose?

Your life's purpose may be different from mine, but I know from my personal experience that fully reconnecting to your childhood ability to live your life with wonder, excitement, intrigue, puzzlement, and the profound satisfaction of loving everyone around you, will add powerful childhood passion to your adult life.

Fortunately, The Wisdom of Children helps us to embrace our childhood ability to love life passionately, as we share ever increasing unconditional love & forgiveness with our friends & family and as we fulfill the unique & special purpose for each of our lives, which makes us worthy of living on Our Precious Mother Earth."

## Challenging What is Untrue

My desire to challenge what is untrue inside

The Imaginary Internal World that I create in my mind

Helps to change my untrue feelings, thoughts & images to the truth

As I navigate The Real External World

In search of the love living

Inside the hearts of my spiritual brothers & sisters

Who are willing to help me

By teaching me how my mind should work

To increase the unconditional love & forgiveness

That I share with everyone in my life

William (Bill) Coulson

www.ingramcontent.com/pod-product-compliance
Lightning Source LLC
Chambersburg PA
CBHW060238050426
42448CB00009B/1501